# Your Faith and You

# Your Faith and You

## A Synthesis of Catholic Belief

James Finley
· Michael Pennock

Ave Maria Press • Notre Dame, Ind. 46556

First printing, May, 1978
Fifth printing, July, 1982
197,000 copies in print

Acknowledgments:

Scipture texts used in this work are taken from the *New American Bible,* copyright © 1970 by the Confraternity of Christian Doctrine and are used by license of the copyright owner.

All quotes of Vatican II documents are taken from *The Documents of Vatican II,* Walter M. Abbott, S.J. (New York: America Press, 1966).

---

Nihil Obstat:
> Rev. Mark A. DiNardo
> Censor Deputatus

Imprimatur:
> Most Rev. James A. Hickey, S.T.D.
> Bishop of Cleveland

Library of Congress Catalog Card Number: 78-53834
International Standard Book Number: 0-87793-153-4

Photography:
> Michael Goldberg, 80; Bob Herbert, 234; Brent Jones, 59; Jean-Claude Lejeune, 25, 112, 134, 151, 174; Robert Maust, 124, 168; Notre Dame Printing and Publications Office, 21, 34, 208; Rick Smolan, cover and 44, 52, 70, 92, 140, 202, 226, 258; David Strickler, 8; Paul Tucker, 192, 220; Wide World Photos, 244.

Printed in the United States of America.

We dedicate this book to our wives Carol Pennock and Kaye Finley. Their love, their concern, and especially their patience made it possible. They have our heartfelt thanks and our love.

# Acknowledgments

It is impossible to thank adequately all the people who have come into our lives and who have helped us in some way in the writing of this book. But we would like to try. First, we want to humbly thank our Lord who has drawn us to do his work and has sustained us in it for the past ten years or so. Teaching religion to young people and adults is a challenge in our contemporary world, but we thank him for the call to try because ours is an exciting, fulfilling profession.

Next, we want to thank our wives, Kaye Finley and Carol Pennock, for putting up with us. Their patience and support have been a source of strength and encouragement. Special thanks to Kaye who typed both drafts of our book.

We want especially to acknowledge all those who have ever taught us. Teaching is a "spiritual" profession—teachers leave a profound and deep impact on their students which time can never erase. We are deeply grateful to those who have helped us develop. We both took master's degrees in religious education at St. John College, Cleveland, Ohio, where we met and were taught by some really great men. We want to thank several of them: George Eppley, the visionary dean of the graduate division—he has been an inspiration to us; Fr. Paul Hritz, one of the best priests in the American Church and our theological mentor; Fr. Mark DiNardo, the Religious Education Director of our diocese, a hard-working leader who has supported us in everything we have done. Our only regret is that St. John's is no longer open to serve others as it has served us.

The following professional colleagues and friends have helped critique the first draft of this book. We are indebted to them. Thanks to Fr. Don Cozzens, PhD, Sr. Cathy Hilkert, OP, Sr. Pat Kozak, CSJ, Fr. Hritz, Sr. Karla Bognar, SND, Fr. Frank Cody, SJ, Philip Kaufman, Esquire and the John T. and Julia A. Spellman Trust, and Rosey Torrence. Their help has been invaluable.

Our students both past and present have been our greatest source of inspiration. It is a joy to teach them; both an honor and a privilege. To all of them we say, thanks. These young men helped us by their insightful comments on our first draft: Mark Doyle, Charles Corrigan, John Galvin, Mike Moran, Dave Debellis, Mike Barrett, Chris Fielding, Greg Kimnach, Dave Mahon, John Znidarsic, Nick Sunyak, Paul Gerace, Pat Hoyer, Dan Riley, Mike Wolfe, Mark Shannon, Rob Kuntz, Rich Soltis, Mark Madigan, Dwayne Bednar, Neil Chambers, Tony Gorsek, Bill Hocter and Ed McCrone.

Our publishers at Ave Maria Press have been great to us. It is providential for us that we were brought together by our friends at Henninger's, Inc., in Cleveland, Ohio. Thanks to Aileen Henninger. And heartfelt thanks to our editor Gene Geissler whose life is a model for us and Charlie Jones whose know-how and concern help keep us going. Marie McIntyre (Pat Kluepfel) of *Religion Teacher's Journal* deserves Mike's deep gratitude for giving him his start. She's a great lady.

Thanks to two Christian communities who have supported us in our work and who nourish us: St. Richard's Parish in North Olmsted, Ohio, Pastor Harry Fagan and our friend, Sr. Mary Naegle, SIW, DRE, and the St. Christopher Parish study group (Rocky River, Ohio).

Finally, thanks to anyone else who has supported and helped us in the writing of this book. God bless you all.

James Finley
Michael Pennock

# Contents

# 1

# God: Our Father

*We believe in one God, the Father almighty, maker of heaven and earth, and of all things visible and invisible.*
(The Nicene Creed)

Has anyone ever asked you what you believe? That is a tough question to answer. The reason it is tough is because we live in an age of unbelief. Many people seem to be cynical and skeptical to a degree never before noticed in human history. They are cautious before putting their faith in anything or anyone. There was a time, for example, when we used to have faith in our athletic heroes, but today many seem to be more interested in their paychecks than in their particular sport or in pleasing the fans. We used to believe in government, but we are now suspicious of every move our leaders make. We used to be able to trust that our cars and stereos and other things would work when we turned them on, but even these mechanical things let us down in this throw-away, built-in-obsolescence age. What can we have faith in anymore?

The question of faith is one of the most important questions we can consider. This is so because beliefs affect our attitudes and actions. In fact, beliefs form our very lives. Beliefs help make us who we are, they reveal what we stand for. This is a book about beliefs which we Catholic Christians hold to be living truth. As a

9

Catholic Christian you are part of a long tradition that goes back to Christ himself. This book is written for you so that you might review what it is we in the Catholic tradition hold to be true about the big questions in life. But a review of our faith is not enough. We must take our faith and do something with it. Faith should lead to action. It is our hope that this basic study of our Roman Catholic faith will help you become more involved in your religion and more in touch with your God.

---

Discuss:
What is the relationship of Catholicism to Christianity?

---

## GOD: THE STARTING POINT

Our starting point is God. People usually start talking about God when they ask the *why* questions. Why am I here? Why is there suffering? Why is there death? Why is there love? Why is there anything at all? Let us pause for a moment and consider what some people think about God. Below you will find a number of statements; you may agree with some, others may make little sense to you. Next to the statement is a scale on which you are to mark your honest reaction of agreement or disagreement: 5 represents total agreement; 1 represents total disagreement. The other numbers represent shades of agreement or disagreement between these two extremes.

---

Statements about God
1. If there is a God, I cannot see how he could possibly be interested in me. I am like a grain of sand in the immensity of the universe. A God would have to be all-powerful, infinite, and so much greater than I. I do not see how he could relate to insignificant me.

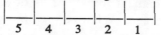

2. God is just an idea that humans have dreamed up to cope with the nothingness beyond death. It would be nice if there were a God, but he is just wishful thinking on our part.

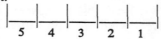

3.  There is a God and he does make a difference. He made
    all things and continues to care for them, including me.
    In short, God is love.

    |—|—|—|—|—|—|
     5   4   3   2   1

4.  If there is a God, how could there be the suffering of
    innocent people, people like little children born maimed,
    war victims, victims of senseless killings, and the like?
    The best argument against God is the existence of evil.

    |—|—|—|—|—|—|
     5   4   3   2   1

5.  You cannot prove there is a God like you can prove
    $1 + 1 = 2$. Until there is that kind of proof, then I
    cannot believe in a God.

    |—|—|—|—|—|—|
     5   4   3   2   1

6.  There might be a God, but so what? What difference
    does he make?

    |—|—|—|—|—|—|
     5   4   3   2   1

7.  The man Jesus is God.

    |—|—|—|—|—|—|
     5   4   3   2   1

8.  God comes in where humans cannot explain things. As
    scientists and others gradually understand more of the
    "mysteries" of life, we find that we need God less. That
    is, we find an explanation for things and he disappears.

    |—|—|—|—|—|—|
     5   4   3   2   1

9.  God is the sum of everything. He is the same as every-
    thing good in the universe put together.

    |—|—|—|—|—|—|
     5   4   3   2   1

10. God is dead.

    |—|—|—|—|—|—|
     5   4   3   2   1


For Discussion:
    Please discuss the following questions in small groups.
    A.  What kind of person would believe in each of these
        descriptions of God?
    B.  Can you disprove any of the statements?
    C.  Which of the above descriptions of God are most
        Christian in your opinion? Why?
    D.  Which do you least agree with and why?

A person cannot escape the question of God. One has to take a stand on God because he is the ultimate question mark in the universe. For example, he comes into the picture whenever people conclude that life is absurd or meaningless. They are confronted by his existence or nonexistence when they experience the death of a parent, when they experience a major setback, when they try to make sense out of war and destructive tornadoes and retarded children.

On the positive side, people turn to God when they contemplate the immensity of the universe on a clear, star-filled night. Or they marvel at the design in creation manifested in inner space, that is, the complexity of the tiniest of particles. The sweet smells of spring, the soft touch of a newborn infant, the experience of a loving embrace given by a friend, the joy of just being alive—all of these make us stop and wonder about the existence of someone (or something) who made it all and keeps it going.

What is the answer to the question of God? For some people the answer is easy. They are either *atheists* or *agnostics*. The *atheist* denies the existence of God. Such a person may have different reasons for rejecting God. Some atheists say that you cannot externally prove that God exists. Others insist that if you believe in God you have downgraded what it means to be a human person. These people say humanity is God, there is no other God. Still others reject belief in the existence of God because they want to protest evil in the world or they claim that there is no spiritual reality, only the material reality of what I can see, taste, touch, smell or hear. Additionally, some people live under governments which reject God and who try to substitute other things or ideas for the real God, things like material wealth and power or economic systems like atheistic communism. Finally, there are the so-called "practical atheists." Practical atheists are those who say they believe in God but this "belief" never affects their lives or values or relationships.

Agnostics, on the other hand, claim that you cannot know there is a God with any degree of certainty. If there is a God, so what?  He can have little interest or influence in the world or in me as an individual.  The agnostic, practically speaking, lives as though there were no God.  His or her prayer goes something like this: "Oh God, if there is a God, save my soul, if I have a soul."

The atheist and the agnostic present a clear challenge to the believer.  They help us reconsider our own belief in God.  They help us clarify in our own lives just exactly who God is and what meaning he has for us.  In this chapter, we will take up the challenge of the nonbeliever and attempt to present an answer to three very important God-questions.  We will answer these questions from the Roman Catholic perspective.  The questions are:

1. Is there a God?
2. If there is a God, does he communicate with us?
3. If he does communicate, what does he have to say?

Discuss:
    Before reading the next section of the chapter, divide in small groups and discuss the three questions listed above.
    Compare and contrast your answers with those of other groups.
          *     *     *     *     *     *     *
The following exercise is intended to help you clarify your present feelings about God.  Do the exercises alone first and then share them with others.  Perhaps the class can come up with a "collective" portrait of God.
.............................................is God's favorite animal which he created because ...........................................................................
God's favorite thing about children is ...................................
.......................................... because ...................................
God's favorite music is ........................................... because ...................................................................
God wants young people to be ...........................................
because ...........................................................
God wants parents to be ...........................................
because ...........................................
God worries most about us when he sees us ........................
.............................................. because ...................................
God's wish for all of us is .......................................................
because ...........................................................

## KEY TEACHINGS

### IS THERE A GOD?

> The wrath of God is being revealed from heaven against the irreligious and perverse spirit of men who, in this perversity of theirs, hinder the truth. In fact, whatever can be known about God is clear to them; he himself made it so. Since the creation of the world, invisible realities, God's eternal power and divinity, have become visible, recognized through the things he has made. Therefore these men are inexcusable.
>
> (Rm 1:18-20)

The above quote of St. Paul suggests rather strongly that all people are able to discover the existence of God by reflecting on the things God has made. The Church teaches in Vatican I "that God, the origin and end of all things, *can be* known with certainty by the natural light of human reason from the things he created." What is the implication of being able to know with certainty the existence of God? For one thing, if you do believe in God, your belief is reasonable. If a person can demonstrate with sufficient certainty that God does indeed exist, then that person need not accept the charge of some atheists who say that people who believe are foolish. If it is reasonable to believe, than it is perhaps foolish not to believe. Secondly, knowing there is a God does give some meaning and purpose to a person's life and to the universe itself. We can know that we are not just freak accidents but are here by someone's design. This in itself gives us hope and some sense of direction.

If we can demonstrate that God does exist, what then are some of the arguments reasonable men and women both within and outside the Catholic Church have used over the centuries which convince them that there is a God? Below four major categories of arguments are presented. The Church has never taught that any one of them is the best argument. One argument may be convincing to some people whereas another may be more persuasive to others. As you read these, try to choose one or two which make some sense to you.

*Personal Experience*

Your own personal experience can help to indicate the existence of God. Your feelings of dependency, your sense of wonder and awe and joy, your feelings of being invited and called to do greater things than you are doing right now—all of these speak of the existence of a Creator. Besides these things, the following help point to God:

- *An insatiable hunger for happiness.* An experience common to all men and women is a craving for happiness. We spend a lot of our time and energy trying to do things and acquire things which will make us happy. For example, we begin our weeks on Monday greatly looking forward to the weekend. Why? Well, the weekend will bring us joy— the dance, the concerts, the sports, the free time. These things make us happy, and yet, do they? Don't they pass all too quickly and make us desire all the more? Are we creatures doomed to ultimate frustration? Or, perhaps, has a Creator made us with an unquenchable thirst for happiness which only he can satisfy? This hunger and thirst have led many people to conclude that there is a Creator who made us humans restless until we rest in him.

- *Sense of justice.* Have you ever felt that the really evil people of the world will someday be called to task? It seems so unfair that the cheaters and liars and killers prosper in this life while some really good people suffer and are taken advantage of. We have a fundamental intuition that things will be reversed someday. We sense in the core of our beings a God who is good and who will right all wrongs if not in this life, then in the next.

- *Love.* How can you explain the greatest reality known to humanity, that is, a sense of being cared for and loved? Love is a spiritual reality which sometimes causes people to sacrifice their lives for others. Material reality cannot explain the existence of love. Where does it ultimately come from if not from LOVE itself, the being we call God? (The same can be said, of course, for intelligence. Matter cannot make intelligence—it must ultimately come from INTELLIGENCE itself, God.)

---

To think about:
    Have you ever had a religious experience which suggested very strongly the existence of God? What did you think about and *feel* during the experience? Afterwards?

---

## Community Experience

Many good and intelligent men and women over the ages have testified to the existence of God. In fact, there is not a culture known to us which did not believe in some being greater than us. Sure, there have been atheistic governments which deny God, but many of the people in those countries still firmly believe in a God. One can argue that such an observation does not "prove" that there is a God. After all, these people may be deceived. This is true, but it is still strong evidence that the common human experience has acknowledged a God, a God who unites, heals and preserves mankind. People have not agreed on who this being is. Some worship him as the sun or as thunder and lightning or some other powerful force. Their disagreement does not disprove the existence of God. These differences merely argue that, left to our own clouded intellects, we cannot clearly perceive God. We have agreed as men and women that someone is out there beyond the stars and in the innermost recesses of our hearts closer to us than we are to ourselves, but the awareness of God becomes easily lost somewhere in our own inner recesses. We need the help of God himself to perceive him more clearly.

## History

The history of mankind is a powerful argument for the existence of God. Where did we intelligent beings come from? What or who has preserved us in often dangerous circumstances? There seems to be an intelligence behind our evolving history, the spread of humanity from the plains of Africa or the Mesopotamian valley to the very ends of the earth and now even to the moon and the outer reaches of the solar system. Is there not a God who is behind all this, leading us on, pulling us up?

*Demonstration Based on Reason*

1. St. Thomas Aquinas, the great medieval Catholic theologian, has presented the so-called five proofs for the existence of God. They all boil down to affirming that we can discover God by looking at what he made. Just like the artist leaves his own personality on the canvas, so, too, God the Creator has left his footprint (so to speak) in the universe which he created. Below is a brief discussion of three of Aquinas' proofs:

> *Uncaused Cause.* Everything we know of in existence was caused by something or someone else. There has to be a source which was the first cause— a first cause which logically always had existence and could not be caused. This first cause is God.

> *The order in nature.* Besides the immensity of the universe (outer space) and the minute intricacy of the tiniest particles of matter (inner space), mankind stands in awe of the laws of nature which rule the entire universe. These laws, that is, the order in nature, must have their source in a supreme Intelligence. This supreme Intelligence we call God.

> *Nothing can explain its own existence.* Nothing that exists came into being of its own accord. At one time, everything that does exist had no existence. But things had to obtain their existence from somewhere—that is, from a Being which, of necessity, had to always exist. That Being which is its own reason for existence we call God.

2. Your own reflection on the beauty, the immensity, the symmetry and the power of creation has probably given you a strong hint of a God who made all things and keeps them in existence. For example, have you ever walked in a dew-drenched woods on a crisp day listening to a babbling brook? What was your reaction? One of wonderment and awe? Or have you walked bare-

foot along a sandy beach on a star-filled night, contemplating the apparent limitlessness of the vast heavens? And on such an occasion, did you marvel at how you, as a small, yet very important part of creation, seem to fit into a grand design planned by a marvelous Being we call God? These reflections of awe and wonderment and marvel point to the existence of God.

**EXERCISES**

1. Have the teacher role play an atheist. Try to convince him/her that there is a God. If an atheist was correct, then what might he/she say about: a. respect for life; b. definition of human life; c. justice; d. the presence of goodness?

2. Divide into five groups. Each group should read one of the following Psalms: 8, 19, 29, 65 or 104. Note what is being praised by the Psalmist. Perhaps the class could make a slide presentation to accompany Psalm 104. Choose appropriate background music. The slide show could be used as a communion meditation.

3. Have someone bring in Beethoven's Sixth (Pastoral) Symphony. With your eyes closed, listen to the first movement. How is Beethoven praising God through his music? Select other appropriate musical selections from contemporary artists.

4. Think about and react to the following: If we compare the age of the earth to one year, then mankind appeared at 8 PM on December 31. Civilization began at a half second before midnight.

5. Our experience can help us understand the nature of God. In the following exercises, please relate your experiences to God, apply your experiences to concepts of God and then discuss each concept of God in light of what you learn in this chapter.

Briefly describe an experience which makes you very happy or which you enjoy very much.
↓
What concept of God could this experience indicate?

Describe a kind of person who you think does the most good or causes the most real happiness to others.
↓
What concept of God does this person evoke?

Describe an event or a scene in nature which fills you with a sense of wonder or awe.
↓
What concept of God does this aspect of nature evoke?

## IF THERE IS A GOD, DOES HE COMMUNICATE WITH US?

> In times past, God spoke in fragmentary and varied ways
> to our fathers through the prophets; in this, the final age,
> he has spoken to us through his Son, whom he has made
> heir of all things and through whom he first created the
> universe.
>
> (Hebrews 1:1-2)

Christians not only believe that there is a God, but they also believe that this God freely communicated himself to mankind, that in his goodness and wisdom, God chose to reveal himself and make known to us the hidden purpose of his will (Vatican Council II). As a result, Christianity is known as a *revealed* religion. The illustrations below might help in understanding the meaning of the term revelation. The first diagram represents humanity separated from God by a veil. God is primarily a mystery to us; his ways are above our ways, his thoughts above our thoughts (Is 55:9). We have already seen, however, that people can discover something about God by looking at his creation. For example, when we look at the vastness of the created universe, we must conclude that he who made it is an infinite being. Or when we discover intelligent human life in creation, we are led to conclude that the Creator must be an intelligent being, the source of human intelligence. But this knowledge of God is veiled or clouded knowledge. People in their natural human condition have only a limited knowledge of God.

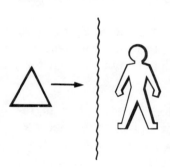

**Diagram 1**
**The invisible God who is mystery is "veiled" (hidden) from total human understanding.**

Our Christian belief is that God freely chose to communicate himself to his creatures. This free gift of God's self-communication is known as supernatural revelation. Technically, revelation means an "unveiling." We believe that on his own initiative, God "unveiled" himself in human history by inviting mankind to share in his very life, by addressing people as friends, by moving among

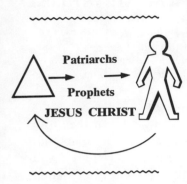

**Diagram 2**
**God "unveils" himself**
**and invites a human**
**response.**

them in order to receive them into his own company. We call this revelation "supernatural" because we, as creatures, do not have a natural right to this intimate relationship with God. His self-disclosure, his invitation to a deeper love and life, is purely a gift on his part.

This story of God's self-disclosure, his saving action in history, is known as *salvation history*. This story has been handed down to the patriarchs, the prophets and the apostles and was interpreted by them and recorded in the Bible. We will consider briefly in the next section of the chapter precisely what was revealed by God in the Old Testament. At this point, we should note that the fullness of God's revelation is his Word made flesh, his Son, Jesus Christ. As Jesus himself proclaims, "I am the way, and the truth, and the life; no one comes to the Father but through me" (Jn 14:6).

As mentioned above, God's revelation invites a human response. That response is known as *faith*. The Epistle to the Hebrews defines faith as the "confident assurance concerning what we hope for, and conviction about things we do not see" (Heb 11:1). Faith, like revelation, is a free gift of God which gives conviction, commitment and trust with regard to realities that can neither be seen clearly nor proved rigorously. Faith is accepting the Lord and his life both by living it and believing it. We get the strength to live and believe God's truth and life from God himself. As Vatican I put it, the source of faith is "the authority of God who reveals . . . , who can neither be deceived nor deceive."

When applied to the Christian, faith is the firm conviction that the meaning of our life and our world is most fully given in the person of Jesus Christ. Our belief is that the Father continues to invite us through the promptings of the Holy Spirit into a loving union with him by way of his Son Jesus Christ who lives and saves all people even today.

For thought and discussion:

1. By looking at creation (revelation through nature or natural revelation), we can discover some things about God. What do the following natural realities tell you about God?
   - a rainbow, waterfall, or sunset
   - a newborn baby
   - the reality of love as shown in a kiss or an embrace
   - mathematical formulae

2. When Moses asked what was the name by which the Israelites should address God, God replied, "I am who am" (Ex 3:14). This name is rendered YAHWEH. What does this name suggest about God's nature? about his relationship to us?

3. How do the following kinds of expressions of faith differ? Are there any similarities?
   a. "I believe in God."
   b. "I believe God."
   c. "I believe that my sick mother will get well."
   d. "I believe in my Honda."
   e. "I believe in you." (Girlfriend to her boyfriend.)
   Are belief and hope related? Explain.

4. Make a list of things and people in which you have faith. Compare/contrast this list with those of your classmates.

5. The first and most important commandment in the Ten Commandments is "I, the Lord, am your God. You shall not have other gods besides me" (Dt 5:6). And yet, many people have other (strange) gods in whom they put their beliefs. These false gods are often the result of false images of God as J. B. Phillips has wisely discussed in his book *Your God Is Too Small*. Listed below are several of these false images of God with a very short explanatory note for each.

   A. *God, the Supercop:* "God is a policeman waiting to catch me in a sin so he can send me to hell."

   B. *God, the Grand Old Man:* "My picture of God is that of a bearded old man whose ideas on how to live are quite old-fashioned."

   C. *God, Absolute Perfection:* "God is so infinite, so perfect that he demands 100% effort on my part, he demands perfection in me. I cannot respond to those kinds of demands."

   D. *God, the Escape Hatch:* "God's major purpose is to serve as my emotional escape hatch. It is good to know he is there in my time of trouble."

E. *God, the General Manager:* "God is so concerned about running the universe, he could not possibly be interested in me."

F. *God, Meek and Mild:* "Religion and belief in God is for the softhearted and sentimental."

• Does Jesus say anything about God which can dispel these false images? (Check your New Testament.)

• Can your personal experience help disprove these false images? (Be sure to give examples.)

• Where do people get these false images of God?

6. How has God communicated to you in your life thus far? By what experiences have you come to recognize or hear him? Are they through people? the Bible? prayer?

---

## IF GOD DOES COMMUNICATE, WHAT DOES HE HAVE TO SAY?

Hear, O Israel! The LORD is our God, the LORD alone! Therefore, you shall love the LORD, your God, with all your heart, and with all your soul, and with all your strength.

(Dt 6:4-5)

We have already discussed that not only is there a God but that he freely chose to reveal and give himself to us. His self-disclosure in human history (known as salvation history) has been recorded in the Bible. This section will discuss Old Testament revelation in five summary points while the next chapter will treat New Testament revelation and Jesus as the high point of God's self-communication. The Old Testament has the following to say about God (and man and woman in relationship to God):

1. *There is only one God.* When God chose to reveal himself to humans he began with the Israelites (Jews). Their history is one of *covenant.* Covenant was a loving relationship entered into between God and the Israelites. In the covenant, God promised to create a people (covenant with Abraham), sustain them as a people (covenant with Moses, the Exodus experience), give them a land (Canaan), establish self-rule (Davidic covenant) and send a Messiah (Davidic covenant).

In return for God's magnificent blessings, the Jews were to obey God's law—a law which gave them a separate identity and a sense of mission. (The law is summarized in the Ten Commandments—Dt 5:6-21 and Ex 20:2-17). The most important aspect of the Israelites' response was to worship Yahweh and testify to him as the one, true God, the source of all being and the one who keeps all creation in existence. All other gods (false) were powerless; only Yahweh is the true, living, unique God. Old Testament history is full of the sad story of how the Israelites were unfaithful to this one, true God and how they continually fell back to the worship of false gods (for example, rain gods or the gods of worldly power and prestige). But the Old Testament also tells a happy story—the story of God's continual loving faithfulness to the forgetful chosen people.

2. *God is a personal loving God, both immanent and transcendent.* The God of the Old Testament is essentially a mystery. As such, he is difficult to categorize. He is both transcendent and immanent. Transcendence refers to the fact that God is totally other than his creation; he is above and beyond it. Immanence refers to the fact that God is present to and joined to his creation. Some religions tend to emphasize one or the other aspect of God's being. For example, Deism (the religion of Benjamin Franklin and Thomas Jefferson) emphasizes God's total otherness, his majesty, and his remoteness from human affairs. The Deists imagine God to be a clockmaker who made the universe, wound it up and then left it alone to run on its own. Other religions like Hinduism are pantheistic. They assert that God is totally immanent, he is in all things; thus, he is all things. Hindus would maintain that the chair you sit on is God—he is not separate from his creation. As the chart below will try to indicate, the God of the Old Testament (and our God, too, since they are the same) reveals himself as both transcendent and immanent. Certain traits emphasize God's majesty and beyondness (transcendence) and other characteristics stress his nearness and concern for mankind (immanence).

## TRANSCENDENCE

1. *Unique.* There is no God like Yahweh. "For thus says the Lord, the creator of the heavens who is God, the designer and maker of the earth who established it, not creating it to be a waste, but designing it to be lived in: I am the Lord, and there is no other." (Is 45:18)

2. *Omnipotent.* God is all-powerful; He can do all things.
For I know that the LORD is great; our Lord is greater than all gods.
All that the LORD wills he does in heaven and on earth, in the seas and in all the deeps.
(Ps 135:5-6)

3. *Eternal.* God always was and always will be. "Do you not know or have you not heard? The Lord is the eternal God, creator of the ends of the earth."
(Is 40:28)

4. *Immensity.* God is not limited to space. "Can it indeed be that God dwells among men on earth? If the heavens cannot contain you, how much less this temple which I have built!"
(1 Kgs 8:27)

## IMMANENCE

1. *Chooses the Hebrews and makes them a people.* "The Lord said to Abram: 'Go forth from the land of your kinsfolk and from your father's house to a land that I will show you. I will make of you a great nation, and I will make your name great, so that you will be a blessing'."
(Gn 12:1-2)

2. *Makes a loving covenant with them.* "Therefore, if you hearken to my voice and keep my covenant, you shall be my special possession, dearer to me than all other people, though all the earth is mine. You shall be to me a kingdom of priests, a holy nation."
(Ex 19:5-6)

3. *Liberates them from Egypt.* "Therefore I have come down to rescue them from the hands of the Egyptians and lead them out of the land into a good and spacious land, a land flowing with milk and honey . . ."
(Ex 3:8)

4. *Gives the Jews a land.* ". . . 'Prepare your provisions, for three days from now you shall cross the Jordan here, to march in and take possession of the Land which the Lord, your God, is giving you.' "
(Jos 1:11)

5. *Contains all things.* "Indeed, she (God's wisdom) reaches from end to end mightily and governs all things well."

(Ws 8:1)

5. *Established the Kingship of David.*
   (See 2 Sam 7:8-16)

6. *Beyond human understanding.* "I (Job) have dealt with great things that I do not understand; things too wonderful for me, which I cannot know."

(Job 42:3)

6. *Sends prophets to guide them.* . . . "Give up your evil ways and keep my commandments and statutes, in accordance with the entire law which I enjoined on your fathers and which I sent you by my servants the prophets," . . .

(2 Kgs 17:13)

7. *Cannot be praised enough.* "Let us praise him the more, since we cannot fathom him, for greater is he than all his works."

(Sir 43:29)

7. *Sustains them in Babylonia and restores them to Israel.*
   (See Is 40:1-2)

In addition, of course, God is a spiritual being. He is a pure spirit who is not made up of matter. God is a personal being, a being who possesses a mind (by which he thinks) and a will (by which he loves).

3. *God is the creator who made all things and keeps them in existence.* The two creation stories (Gn 1:1-2:4 and Gn 2:5-25) reveal that God is the creator. He made all things out of nothing. He created freely out of his great generosity. He both sustains and rules the world. The apex of God's creation is mankind. "God created man in his image; in the divine image he created him; male and female he created them (Gn 1:27)." All that he created was good (Gn 1:30).

These Genesis creation stories reveal a good and powerful and generous God. Unlike the Babylonian creation stories which maintain that there is an evil god along with a good god or that man's existence is the result of evil, the Old Testament picture of God is one of goodness, freedom and generosity. The crown of God's creation, mankind, is presented as having both a physical body and a spiritual nature. Mankind's spiritual nature enables him to think, to choose between right and wrong, and to love. Man is immortal, that is, though he had a beginning, individual men and women will never cease to exist. Humans are social beings ("male and female he created them") who live in community. Their task is to renew the face of the earth. "God blessed them, saying: 'Be fertile and multiply; fill the earth and subdue it. Have dominion over the fish of the sea, the birds of the air, and all the living things that move on the earth' " (Gn 1:28).

4. *Sin brings unhappiness which results from man's failure to love.* Old Testament revelation shows why there is evil in the world. (See, for example, Gn 3.) In the Adam and Eve story we see that originally mankind was in harmony with God, that is, on friendship terms. But because God desired to create free beings (not puppets), humans had the chance to either accept or reject God's love. Original sin is the unhappy story of Adam and Eve's free rejection of God's love, their failure to love, which resulted in humanity's loss

of Yahweh's friendship. This lack of unity between God and ourselves also brought about a corresponding disharmony between ourselves and nature and alienation from other people. All future
generations after our first parents inherited original sin and its
effects.

5. *God wills not only to forgive the sins of people, but to
establish mankind in peace and happiness forever.* As we mentioned already, part of the story of salvation history is God's incredible loving faithfulness to his unfaithful creatures. For example,
the prophet Hosea compares Yahweh to a faithful husband who
refuses to abandon his harlot wife Israel (see Hos 2). The beautiful
Song of Songs presents Yahweh as a passionate lover whose love
and fidelity to his wife (Israel) know no bounds.

God's love is manifested through deeds as well as words. His
deeds reflect a God who saves, one who rescues the Jews from the
bondage of slavery in Egypt, one who sustains them in the desert,
one who gives them a land and a king, one who keeps them alive
in captivity, one who returns them to their land.

The high point of God's loving concern is his promise to send
a Messiah, a savior, a comforter who will restore mankind to a
proper relationship with God.

> But you, Bethlehem-Ephrathah
>     too small to be among the clans of Judah,
> From you shall come forth for me
>     one who is to be ruler in Israel;
> Whose origin is from of old,
>     from ancient times. (Mi 5:1)

Yahweh sent his only Son, Jesus Christ. This is part of the
New Testament story discussed in Chapter 2.

---

For further Reflection:

1. Read these two Messianic prophecies: 2 Sam 7:3-16
   and Amos 9:11-15. What do they clarify about the
   prophecy from Micah quoted above?

2. Research the creation stories of the ancient Egyptians, Babylonians and the Greeks. (Perhaps for contrast, you might wish to look into the stories of an American Indian tribe, too.) Compare/contrast their treatment of the creation of mankind and the world with that found in the two Genesis accounts. Discuss the following points:

   a. Mankind's origin
   b. The origin of women
   c. Goodness or evilness as the source of creation
   d. The source of evil

3. Please read the following Scripture passages: Lam 5: 17-20; Ps 139:6; Jer 10:10-12; Is 55. Which trait from the chart on transcendence does each passage most nearly describe?

4. God loves us passionately, too. How do you think of him when you approach the sacrament of reconciliation? A king? a judge? a loving father? a friend?

## WHAT DOES THIS MEAN?

This chapter has presented some basic Catholic teachings on God, especially as he has revealed himself in the Old Testament. Your initial reaction might be one of "Well, that's nice, but what real difference do these truths make in my life?" That is a good question and one that ought not too easily be dismissed. Young people are so busy growing up and discovering wonderful things about life and human relationships that sometimes God is the farthest thing from their minds. But, nevertheless, it is worthwhile to pause periodically and consider what impact God does have on us at the various stages of our lives. Below are listed a few observations which may help to make these teachings about God more real to you at this point in your life.

- For one thing, we observed that God is incredibly good and loving. He shows this goodness by making all of creation, including us. This is a powerful truth that has widespread ramifications. It means, in brief, that you are loved by him unconditionally. He brought you into existence and gave you certain talents and he sees that what he made is good, very good. Others may put guilt trips on us that we are not good unless we measure up to their expectations. *With God, we do not have to play games.* He loves us for who we are. After all, he made us. If we let this knowledge sink into the core of our inner awareness, we should be joyful about ourselves and life itself.

- Life does have meaning, even in its most confusing moments. Sometimes we all feel like "hanging it up," "giving up," "copping out." But our faith helps us realize that, basically, reality is good, that things will work out because our God is good and he cares. God's creation reveals that after every dark night, there is a glorious sunrise. So, too, because God cares for us, a bright dawn will follow.

- This history of the Old Testament shows that God likes to get involved in our lives. The most obvious way is that he is everywhere, thus he is closer to us than we are to ourselves. But he promised the Jews that he would never abandon them and he did not. He was faithful to his word. His promise to us is that he will never abandon us, regardless of how we sin or turn from his love. His generous love is always there ready for us to embrace. This is great news because it helps us know that no matter what terrible things we do, God's love will be there and even hound us to the ends of the earth.

---

For Discussion and Reflection:

1. Do you agree with the three observations above? Do you find it liberating not to have to prove how worthwhile you are to God? How prevalent in our society do you think is the pressure of having to prove our worth in the eyes of others? Is this always a bad thing?

2. The second observation claims that eventually things work out, no matter how bleak they look now. Do you have any experience that bears this out?

3. Can you add to the above list of observations?

4. Thinking about God and his goodness often leads us to prayer where we lift up our minds and hearts to God. You might find the following helpful:

a. Read reflectively several of the Psalms of praise: 8; 19; 29; 33; 46; 65; 76; 84; 105; 111; 113; 114; 117; 122; 135; 136; 145-150.

b. Write your own prayer of thanksgiving to God for his creation and other gifts he has granted to you. You may wish to illustrate with drawings, pictures and the like.

c. Keep a brief journal in which you observe at the end of each day how God worked in your life that day.

d. Alone, take a "nature walk" and "listen for God." (Can you find him in the hustle and bustle of cities, too?)

---

## ADDITIONAL QUESTIONS:

Young people often ask the following questions about God which have not been discussed above. We will provide a brief response to them here.

1. *If God knows all things, even what I am going to do in the future, does this not take away my freedom, that is, predetermine me?*

No, it does not! Why not? God's knowledge does not *force* me to do anything. In his love, he made me free. He respects that freedom, even if the freedom leads me away from his love. There is no cause-effect relationship between his knowledge and my actions. Here is an analogy which might help clarify this point: You are on the fifth floor of a building looking down on the street below. You see a friend crossing the street. You also see a car coming. You know that the car will hit your friend, it is inevitable if she keeps crossing the street. She gets hit by the car. Your pre-knowledge did not cause the accident or force your friend to cross. So it is with God.

*2. If God is good, then why is there evil in the world?*

Evil is a great mystery. In fact, some people claim that religion is an attempt to reconcile good and evil in the universe. The answer to this question again revolves around a loving God who makes not puppets but intelligent beings with freedom. God does not create evil; evil is the absence of good. Rather, God permits evil. Evil enters the picture when free, intelligent creatures, both angels and humans, turn from God's love. Some evil is easy to understand. For example, it is easy to see how abortions of innocent babies, prejudice and the terrible consequences it causes, and war come from man's deliberate choice to turn from a loving God. Our belief, too, is that some evil in the universe results from fallen angels (devils) at odds with their Creator. Other kinds of evil are simply beyond our human understanding.

## SUMMARY

The following points help to sum up this chapter.

1. An atheist denies that God exists; an agnostic maintains that if there is a God he makes little practical difference.

2. Christians believe there is a God and that human reason can discover him by reflecting on nature, one's personal experience, the experience of the community and human history.

3. We believe that God freely chose to share his life with his creatures. We call this revelation. Jesus is the high point of God's self-disclosure. Faith is man's response to God's revelation.

4. The God of the Old Testament revelation reveals the following about himself and mankind:

   a. His traits: one, true, living, unique, omnipotent, eternal, immense, contains all things, beyond human

understanding, a pure spirit, an absolute loving being
who is concerned intimately with his creation.

b. His relationship to us: He creates all things out of
nothing and keeps them in existence. He has made
man in his image and likeness with a supernatural
destiny. He desires the happiness of all people. He is
faithful to us even when we are not.

c. The story of mankind is one of sin and the rejection
of God's love, but God stands ready to redeem mankind through his Son, Jesus.

## EVALUATION:

Please turn to the first exercise of the chapter entitled, "Statements
about God." In light of this chapter, discuss and criticize each of
the positions made. Have any of your own personal opinions
changed because of this chapter?

### FURTHER ACTIVITIES:

1. Write an essay entitled "What God Means to Me."

2. Interview the following kinds of people to get their
reaction to the question "Who is God?": brothers and
sisters, parents, friends, favorite teacher, a couple of
strangers.

3. Research the teaching about God in the following religions: Hinduism, ancient Canaanite religion, an American Indian tribe, an Australian aborigine tribe, the
God of Taoism.

4. Watch several popular TV shows which deal with life-
and-death issues. Discuss:

   a. Do these shows deny God? Ignore him?
   b. Do they tend to take a Deistic approach, that
   is, there is a God, but he has little to do with
   our lives?
   c. Do they ridicule religion by poking fun at
   religious beliefs or do they merely ridicule it by
   ignoring it? Do they promote an antireligious
   attitude? Discuss.

5. Read one of the following books and make a report on
   it:

> Donald P. Gray, *Where Is Your God?* (Dayton:
> Pflaum, 1969).
>
> Andrew Greeley, *What a Modern Catholic Be-
> lieves About God* (Chicago: Thomas More,
> 1971).
>
> Christopher Kiesling, *Any News of God?* (Day-
> ton, Pflaum, 1970).
>
> J.B. Phillips, *Your God Is Too Small* (New York:
> The Macmillan Co., 1970).

# 2

# Jesus

*Continue therefore to live in Christ Jesus the Lord, in the spirit in which you received him. Be rooted in him and built up in him, growing ever stronger in faith. . . .*

(Col 2:6-7)

A Christian is, above all, a disciple of Jesus Christ. The risen Jesus gives meaning, strength and reality to all that the Church believes and teaches. Surely then, the most critical question we Catholics can ask ourselves is "Who is Jesus?"

**Who is Jesus?**

Provide three answers to each of the following questions. Place your answers to each question in the order of importance which conforms to your present understanding of who Jesus is. The class may combine the answers to form a kind of summary of its beliefs about Jesus.

Who is Jesus?_____

What did Jesus teach?_____

How are we united to Jesus?_____

What difference does Jesus make in the lives of those who believe in him?_____

In this chapter we will be studying about Jesus under the following headings:

1. The historical Jesus
2. Who is Jesus? The response of faith
3. Jesus: His cross and resurrection
4. Jesus: True God and true man
5. The teachings of Jesus


## THE HISTORICAL JESUS

Of course, neither the Jews nor the Romans of Jesus' day kept the detailed records and statistics that we do today. But to help us with our purposes here of learning about the historical Jesus, imagine that you are a Roman official assigned the task of filling in Jesus' death certificate. In doing the exercise do not make up any answers. Rather, leave blank any spaces that cannot be filled in. The following passages may help you when and if you get stuck: Mt 1-2; Lk 1-2; Jn 18-19.

```
+---------------------------------------------------------------+
|                    DEATH CERTIFICATE                          |
|                                                               |
| NAME_____ Height_____ Age____          |
| Aliases_____ Eye Color_____ Sex____         |
| Father's Name_____Mother's Name_____         |
| City of Birth_____Occupation _____          |
| Permanent Address_____         |
| Properties owned at time of death_____         |
| Crime committed_____         |
| Cause of death_____         |
| Date/Time of death_____         |
| Burial details_____         |
+---------------------------------------------------------------+
```

Doing the above exercise helps us appreciate how little we know about the external details of Jesus' life: What did Jesus look like? How, exactly, did he spend the first thirty years of his life? How did he talk, walk and laugh? These and countless other similar details are not given to us in the gospels.

But the gospels do tell us enough about the historical Jesus to make one thing quite clear: we cannot answer the question "Who is Jesus?" without saying that Jesus was a *real, historical* human being. He was a man born at a definite time and place (Mt 1-2; Lk 1-2:21). He grew up and matured more or less like many other Jewish boys of his day (Lk 2:39-40). Even after Jesus began his public ministry displaying his totally unique identity and mission he, nevertheless, remained historically real and human. He displayed emotion (Mk 11:15-19; Lk 19:41-44). He knew fatigue (Jn 4:6). He took part in the social life of his day (Jn 2:1-2; Lk 22:7-8). Finally, in the face of danger, he experienced genuine fear (Mt 26:36-46). And, in the end, he experienced pain (Mt 27:27-31). Jesus was, then, no legendary or mythical figure. He was a human being, one of us in every way except sin.

## A Portrait of the Historical Jesus

As noted above, the gospels reveal little about Jesus' appearance or the external details of his daily life. But the gospels do provide us with many little glimpses into Jesus' personality by revealing to us the way he interacted with those around him. We note, for example, that Jesus often physically touched those around him, as, for example, when he touched a leper in order to cure him (Mt 8:1-4) or when he touched the confused and frightened disciples after the transfiguration (Mt 17:1-8). We note, too, that Jesus often displayed great courage as when he boldly stopped a group of men who were about to stone to death the woman caught in adultery (Jn 8:1-11). So, too, when Jesus washed his disciples' feet he reveals to us that he was humble (Jn 13:1-17). His statements regarding the poor widow's offering reveal that he was keenly observant of the hidden greatness of those unnoticed by others (Lk 19:13-15).

---

Draw your own portrait of Jesus by selecting a gospel story and relating what you think it tells us about what *kind of person* Jesus was. These "portraits" should be shared and the class can attempt to put together some kind of general statement describing the most significant aspects of Jesus' personality.

---

## WHO IS JESUS?

In one of the opening chapters of the gospel according to Matthew we hear of Jesus standing up in the synagogue before the gathered community and reading these words from the prophet Isaiah:

> The spirit of the Lord is upon me;
>     therefore he has anointed me.
> He has sent me to bring glad tidings to the poor,
>     to proclaim liberty to captives,
> Recovery of sight to the blind
>     and release to prisoners,
> To announce a year of favor from the Lord.
>                                   —(Lk 4:18-19)

Luke continues by adding that Jesus closed the scroll and announced to his listeners, "Today this scripture passage is fulfilled in your hearing." In response to this the crowd "marveled." They understood something of what Jesus was trying to say; namely, that he himself was the fulfillment of all the Old Testament hopes and prophecies. This implied much more than being simply a wise teacher or a gentle lover of the poor. It implied that Jesus was, in fact, the long-awaited Messiah, the redeemer of Israel.

In the Jesus of history we find a very attractive, unusual man who had a deep influence on the lives of those who knew him. But in the Christ of faith, that is, in Christ as seen through the eyes of Old Testament hope for salvation, we find in Jesus God himself giving us his life and his love in the person of his Son Jesus.

This vital point takes us to the true, inner meaning of the gospel stories about Jesus. When Jesus gave the blind their sight, made the deaf to hear or the lame to walk he was offering us external signs of *inner healing* that comes to us through *faith*. By faith in Jesus, our eyes are opened to see that Jesus is our Life and that he is present in those around us. Our ears are opened to hear Jesus and to hear him speaking to us in the voice of those in need. We are able to walk to Jesus and go to him present in the neglected and forgotten. Thus, being a disciple of Jesus means much more than believing he was a good man. It means personally putting one's faith in him as the source of one's life and happiness. The Christ of faith is the Christ we discover not by turning to history but by prayer and by trying daily to live like Jesus in order to become ourselves sources of his presence to those around us.

---

**ACTIVITIES:**

1. In the Exodus story God leads his people through the desert to the promised land. He becomes the sole source of their *life*. His saving action points out to them their *way* out of bondage and death. He gives them *water* from a rock. He guides them at night by a light from heaven. He feeds them with bread from heaven (Ex 13:21-22, 16-17).

   Compare these elements of the Exodus story with Jesus' statement that: "I am the *way,* the truth, and the *life"* (Jn 14:6).

   that:

   > "I am the light of the world.
   > No follower of mine shall ever walk in darkness;
   > no, he shall possess the light of life" (Jn 8:12).

   that:

   > "I myself am the bread of life.
   > No one who comes to me shall ever be hungry" (Jn 6:35).

   and that:

   > "But whoever drinks the water I give him will never be thirsty" (Jn 4:14).

   What do these comparisons tell you about the Gospel's proclamation of the importance of Jesus in our lives? Has he become this vital in your life?

2. Israel had her sacred history, her story, in which she was able to see God's saving action which was to find its perfection in Christ. Reflect on your own "private history," that is, the past experiences of your life. In what ways do you think it means to say that Christ is the center of your life, that all the experiences of your life should be seen in the light of Christ?

3. Commercials and ads try to substitute false values or create false needs in order to sell their product. Many of these are takeoffs on the "way, life, light and water" themes found in the gospels. Below are listed several of these. Add to the list and then discuss how every product or service ultimately frustrates people who are searching for real values, real life.

*Examples:*

> Pepsi's got a lot to give.
> Go the United Way.
> Salem ad: "I don't let anything get in the way of my enjoyment."
> Ad for wine: "Love in a round bottle."

## THE CROSS AND RESURRECTION

By their response to the historical Jesus the disciples demonstrated their faith in him as the awaited Redeemer of Israel. What the disciples were not prepared for was the full extent of God's saving action by which he, through Christ, would unite humanity to himself.

In the eighth chapter of Mark's Gospel, Jesus tells his disciples that he must suffer and be put to death. The disciples, filled with awe and reverence for Jesus as the Messiah, are shocked by Jesus' words. But Jesus goes on not only to insist upon his own death but to say that the disciples too must *share* in his death if they are to share in the *life,* the *light,* and joy he came on earth to give them. Jesus says:

> If a man wishes to come after me, he must deny his very self, take up his cross, and follow in my steps. Whoever would preserve his life will lose it, but whoever loses his life for my sake and the gospel's will preserve it.
>
> (Mk 8:34-35)

Following these words of Jesus, Mark tells us about Jesus' transfiguration (Mk 9:2-13) when Jesus became marvelously transformed before the disciples' eyes. This close relationship between Jesus' talk of the cross and his glorious transfiguration became reenacted with an utter finality when Jesus was crucified and then three days later rose from the dead.

Once again, the gospels are not primarily concerned about the external details of Jesus' crucifixion. And they tell us no one was present to observe the actual moment of Jesus' resurrection within the tomb. But what the gospels do stress is that both Jesus' death and resurrection are very real. Jesus truly died and he now truly lives.

Furthermore, the gospels stress that the meaning of Jesus' death is that by his death Jesus gave us life. He, through his cross, put to death all that can possibly separate us from God. The *meaning* of Jesus' death is life for us. The resurrection is the great sign of this new eternal life given to us in and through the power of the resurrected Jesus. For Jesus not only rose but he himself promised that we too will rise if we *respond* to him in *faith* and live out that faith in the way we live our daily lives. In fact, he told us that the reason why he rose was precisely to give us a share in his own eternal life with the Father (Jn 14-17). He rose not for himself but for us.

---

For Discussion:

As a class discuss how each of the following situations calls for a kind of little "death" to selfishness and at the same time offers a kind of little "resurrection" of inner peace and wholeness.

A brother or sister who wants to see his/her favorite TV show at the same time your favorite show is on.

At a time you are feeling tired, a friend calls on the phone and expresses the need to talk.

A parent who lets it be known that he/she sincerely wants to learn to communicate better with you.

A school program that calls for volunteers to help direct a canned food drive for the poor at Christmas.

After reflecting on these and other similar occasions as moments in which we can share in Christ's death and resurrection, discuss the need for prayer, that is, the need for personal union with Christ in order to find the strength to live like Christ.

Of course, Christ died and rose not simply for these little moments of spiritual life experienced in our daily efforts to live like him. Be sure to discuss as a class, too, the importance of eternal life understood as life that follows biological death.

## JESUS HUMAN AND DIVINE

The first few centuries of the Church's existence were marked by much growth not only in terms of numbers but also in terms of understanding who Jesus is and what he achieved for us by his life, death and resurrection. Those Church leaders who wrote during this period are called the *Fathers of the Church*. To this day the Church still draws upon the wisdom and beauty of their words.

But during this same period some (no doubt, sincere) people began presenting ideas that attacked the basis of Christian faith in Jesus. These erroneous ideas, called heresies, took many forms. But they can be divided into two main groups with respect to their teaching about Jesus. One group denied that Jesus was a real human being. Thus, he did not truly live our human life, suffer and die on the cross for us. The second group denied that Jesus was divine, that is, that he was truly God. These heresies proved to be the occasion for the Church to further clarify her belief about Jesus. In order to do this the bishops of the Church came together to meet in Councils. There were four main Councils during this period: Nicaea (325), Constantinople (381), Ephesus (431) and Chalcedon (451). The conclusions of these Councils, in terms of our study here, can be summarized as follows:

1. There is only one *person* in Jesus. This is a divine Person, the second Person of the Trinity.

2. There are two natures in Jesus. He had a *Divine Nature,* for he was *God*. And he also had a *human nature*.

3. The union of the human and Divine natures in the Person of Jesus is so perfect that we must say that, in Jesus, God truly shared our life with us,

truly suffered, truly underwent death, and truly
rose victorious over death.

4. Jesus the God-man went through human life,
   suffering and death solely for our salvation. By
   uniting ourselves to his death through faith we
   find our new eternal share in his resurrection.

---

Since the Council of Chalcedon, the Creed formulated at
the Council of Nicaea has been considered the most com-
monly accepted creedal statement of the Church about
Jesus. Read slowly through the parts of the Creed given
below and pinpoint those statements which affirm the
divinity of Jesus and those statements which affirm his
humanity.

> **We believe in one Lord, Jesus Christ**
> **the only Son of God,**
> **eternally begotten of the Father,**
> **God from God, Light from Light,**
> **true God from true God,**
> **begotten, not made, one in Being with the**
> **Father.**
> **Through him all things were made.**
> **For us men and for our salvation**
> **he came down from heaven:**
> **by the power of the Holy Spirit**
> **he was born of the Virgin Mary, and**
> **became man.**
>
> **For our sake he was crucified under Pontius**
> **Pilate:**
> **he suffered, died, and was buried.**
> **On the third day he rose again**
> **in fulfillment of the Scriptures;**
> **he ascended into heaven**
> **and is seated at the right hand of the**
> **Father.**
> **He will come again in glory**
> **to judge the living and the dead,**
> **and his kingdom will have no end.**

## WHAT DID JESUS TEACH?

Rank the items below in order of importance to you, that
is, how much time you spend thinking about them.

       ——   relationship with the opposite sex
       ——   my future
       ——   how popular I am
       ——   how others treat me
       ——   mistakes I've made
       ——   my relationship with God
       ——   my relationship with my parents
       ——   money
       ——   my relationships and reactions to others

A great deal of the teaching of Jesus is contained in the
Sermon on the Mount, Mt 5-7. Read the Sermon and then
discuss with your classmates how you think Jesus would
want us to react to each of the points listed above.

Once we grasp something of who Jesus is we can then turn to his teachings with the ears of a disciple. Jesus once accused the Pharisees saying, "You have eyes to see and do not see and ears to hear and do not hear." What he meant, of course, is that it is not enough just to hear the surface meaning of his words. We must penetrate into the depths of what Jesus teaches us. We must sense the power and the importance of what he tells us. And we can do this once we sense in faith what it is Jesus is speaking to us.

---

People say "love is blind." But in what sense can we say that only in love can we "see" the other person, and that only in friendship and love can we "hear" what the other is saying? In this respect, what does it mean not to "hear" a friend? What does all of this tell us about the need for love and faith in our efforts to hear Jesus?

---

What follows is a brief summary of most of the main elements of Jesus' teaching. What was said above about the need to have faith in order to hear Jesus' words should help us realize the inadequacy of a summary such as this. Each of us needs to learn to read the New Testament with an open mind and heart. We need to read the New Testament in an attitude of faith and prayer to hear what Jesus is telling us through the words of scripture. Likewise, during Mass we need to really listen to the reading of God's word. Nothing can replace this kind of listening. The value of a book like this and the summary that follows is that they can aid you in understanding your faith. They can help you gain an overall synthesis or overview of your faith. But, of course, it is only in a sincere prayer encounter with Jesus that your faith can develop and grow in a way that can actually change your life.

*Jesus: The Way, the Truth, and the Life.* Jesus taught his disciples about himself. He taught that those who believe in him and become his disciples will find eternal life. Jesus *was sent by God to heal us and make us full sharers in Jesus' own life with the Father.* (Jn 6; Jn 14)

*Abba, Father.* Jesus taught that God is not an impersonal force like gravity, not a ruthless lawgiver.

But rather, God is *our Father who loves us with a tender love that utterly surpasses our understanding.* He loved us so much he even sent us his only son to die for us that we might have life. (Mt 6:9; Lk 15:11-32)

*Love of God and Neighbor:* Jesus gave his love freely and taught that the essence of our response to Abba was love. The greatest commandment, he said, was to love the Lord your God with your whole heart, soul and mind (Mt 22:37). The next greatest commandment?

You shall love your neighbor as yourself.
(Mt 22:39)

*We Have Been Given the Holy Spirit.* Jesus taught that he would be with us always for he would send to us the Holy Spirit. *The Holy Spirit is God as he dwells within us. The Spirit puts us in a profound relationship of intimacy with Jesus.* The Spirit guides, strengthens us and makes us holy. It is the Spirit who gives us the power to believe in Jesus and offer our life to him. (Jn 16:7-26; Acts 2)

*The Gift of Life Is An Invitation.* Christ calls us to respond to the gift of life he offers us. He invites us to a life of faith which is our personal acceptance of him as the Lord and Savior of our lives. We must freely choose to be Christ's disciples if his life, death and resurrection are to bear fruit in our lives. (Mk 1:14-22)

*The Disciple Must Live Like Christ.* United to Christ in the Spirit the disciple must respond to Christ by a living faith. The disciple's *attitudes* and *actions* must be a witness to Christ. Others must be able to meet Christ living in those who believe in him. This means treating others as our brothers and sisters in Christ. (Mt 5-7; Jn 15:9-17)

*To Live Like Christ Is to Share in the Cross and Resurrection.* Our daily hardship and losses, failures and frustrations and eventually even our death must be seen as the ways we share in Christ's cross.

We must, above all, share in his cross by trying as best we can to renounce all sinful actions and attitudes from our life. This burden of the cross is in fact "light and easy," for Christ gives his followers through the cross a share in the peace and joy of his resurrection. (Mt 10:38; Rom 6)

*The Kingdom of God Will Come.* Jesus taught that one day God himself will radically intervene in human history. God will transform the earth and unite all men and women everywhere into the perfect, eternal social unity of love and justice that Jesus called the Kingdom of God. Jesus came to announce that his coming had already begun this kingdom on earth. The disciples of Jesus must prepare for the coming of the Kingdom when Christ will visibly return in glory to judge the living and the dead. (Mt 13:1-52; 20:1-16)

---

What Did Christ Say About . . .

Listed below are a number of assorted topics. First discuss what you think about the topic, then what you think Christ taught about it. Then, look up the text indicated to find out what Christ taught. Discuss Christ's teaching together as a class.

| Life After Death | Sin | Money |
|---|---|---|
| Jn 6 | Mt 5-7;<br>Lk 11:17-23 | Mt 5:42;<br>Lk 12:14-34 |

| Prayer | Faith | Marriage/<br>Divorce |
|---|---|---|
| Mt 6:5, 7:7-11;<br>Lk 11:5-13;<br>Jn 14:13-14 | Mt 6:25, 34,14<br>27-31, 17:20-21;<br>Mk 11:14, 22-26 | Mt 19:4-12<br>Mk 10:3-12 |

---

## WHAT DOES THIS MEAN?

What difference does all this talk about Jesus mean in your life? To answer this question we must pause to consider that during his lifetime Jesus confronted many people with his invitation to believe in him. Some rejected Christ outright and even turned against him. Many others simply shrugged their shoulders and walked away without ever facing squarely the decision Jesus invited them to make. The disciples of Christ were men and women who heard Christ speak, pondered his words in their hearts and then made a personal acceptance of him into their lives.

The truth of Jesus stands forever whether we accept it or not. But within our daily experience Jesus makes no difference until we personally turn to him and accept him into our lives. The following points are offered as the most important difference Jesus makes in our lives once we accept him in faith.

- Regardless of how we feel, regardless of how bleak life may seem, the ultimate, underlying reality of all life is that of God who is a loving Father. He is one we can call *Abba* (Daddy). His love for us knows no bounds. It is always radically beyond anything we can imagine.

- All of our own weakness and sinfulness, all the evil in the world around us has been *healed* by God through Christ's death and resurrection. Our union with Christ is so close that he himself becomes our goodness and our hope. In Christ God has judged all of us and he has judged us with forgiveness. We have but to accept this forgiveness by a genuine response of faith in Christ and continually strive to grow in our daily fidelity to Christ by avoiding sin in our life.

- Jesus fully entered into human life and transformed it from within. So, too, we must not hold back from giving ourselves to others in love and service. We must fully enter into our home life, our school life, our friendships, our hopes and dreams. We must live our human life to the fullest and help others to do the same. For Jesus has made this human life we live his own. We must too, in turn, find in Christ the ultimate meaning and purpose of all we do and experience.

- Even death itself offers no threat to the life that has been given to us in Christ. We must trust and believe that all the good things God has given us in this life are but faith promises of what he has in store for us.

For Discussion and Reflection:

1. Do you agree with the above observations? Do you find the idea of being a disciple of Christ appealing? Have you ever met anyone who especially impressed you as being a true disciple of Christ?

2. Can you add to the list of observations given above?

3. What *attitudes* do you think are essential to develop faith in Christ? What *attitudes* do you think make it difficult for one to grow in faith in Christ? What elements of our society today contribute to growing in faith in Christ? What elements hinder it?

4. Read the parable of the sower casting his seed (Mt 13:4-12). Can you think of concrete examples of kinds of people and situations which correspond to each kind of ground on which the seed fell?

5. Write a letter to Christ telling him what difference he has made so far in your life and why.

## OTHER QUESTIONS

Given below is a question which young people frequently ask about Jesus.

*How do we know Jesus is real? Maybe the disciples just made up or imagined all they said about him.*

We can point to the *historical* reality of Jesus by realizing that: 1. Some pagan sources such as Josephus and Tacitus refer to Jesus as a historical figure. 2. Archeologists are finding more and more artifacts which support stories as told in the gospels. 3. The disciples stood to gain nothing by making up a Jesus story. In fact, all but John were put to death rather than deny all they said about Jesus. 4. The gospels ring with an air of depth, clarity and sincerity that seems to rule out the possibility of their being written either as a hoax or by half-insane men who imagined something that never happened.

As to the Christ of *faith,* the resurrection, and Jesus' claim to offer life to all who believe in him, we must realize that we are basically in the same position as the first disciples. We face a decision to either believe or not believe Jesus and his message of salvation. There is strong evidence to support the reality of the historical Jesus, his strength and his depth as a person. This evidence helps us see the basis for belief in what Jesus said. But the faith itself in him is a gift of the Holy Spirit. Each of us must make this act of faith as a free adult. There is no "proof" that takes away the challenge and the risk of faith. But once we do believe in Jesus then each of us can experience the reality and power of his presence in our life. But even this presence is not something we prove but rather live and for which we are grateful.

## SUMMARY

The following points summarize what was covered in this chapter.

1. Jesus was a real, historical figure. We can learn much about him by carefully reading the gospels.

2. The Good News of the gospel is that the man, Jesus, is in fact the Son of God who gives us life through his death and resurrection.

3. To have the life Christ offers us we must become his disciples by having faith in him, converting our whole life over to him by living according to his will, and sharing in his cross by renouncing sin in our lives. In this way we come to share in his resurrection.

4. The early Councils of the Church proclaim that Jesus is the God-man, one divine person with both a human and a divine nature.

5. Jesus taught: He is the source of life; God is a loving Father; the Holy Spirit dwells in us giving us the power to believe in Jesus; the disciple must *live* like Christ by loving God and others as Christ did. To live like Christ we must share in his cross and resurrection; to live in this way is to prepare for the coming of the Kingdom of God.

## EVALUATION

Please turn to the opening exercise of this chapter entitled "Who Is Jesus?" In light of this chapter, discuss and criticize the answers you gave in class. What changes has this chapter made in your own personal opinions about Jesus?

### FURTHER ACTIVITIES

1. Write an essay entitled "What Jesus Means To Me."

2. Select several currently popular television shows and evaluate them in the light of Christ. Do they support Christian values and attitudes? Are they indifferent to them or do they perhaps even oppose Christian values, for example, the sacredness of life?

3. Read through the litany of the Sacred Heart of Jesus and the litany of the Holy Name of Jesus. Discuss some of the titles given to Jesus. A Bible concordance or a copy of the *Jerome Biblical Commentary* will prove helpful in researching the titles given to Jesus.

4. Interview parish priests, teachers, family members about what Christ means to them. Write up the interview for posting in the classroom.

5. The class can rent a film on Jesus such as *King of Kings,* or listen to records of *Jesus Christ, Superstar* or *Godspell.* How would you characterize these reactions to Jesus? Discuss the portrayal of Jesus in the highly acclaimed TV movie, Zeffirelli's *Jesus of Nazareth.*

6. Read the life of a saint. Report on the way Christ totally transformed the saint's life.

7. Have as a guest speaker someone who has recently turned his/her life over to Jesus. This person might give a witness talk on what Jesus means in his or her life.

# 3

# The Trinity and the Holy Spirit

*. . . by the power of the Holy Spirit he was born of the virgin Mary and became man.*

(The Nicene Creed)

This chapter begins with a study of the Trinity. We have already learned about the Father in Chapter I and about the Son in Chapter II. In this chapter we will emphasize the Holy Spirit as we explore the mystery of God's Trinitarian life and the way in which each person of the Trinity is active in our daily lives.

---

**Exercise:**

In order to get us thinking about how each of the persons of the Trinity is active in our life, pause to reflect on your present notions of God's presence.

The following exercise lists six moments when you might feel God's presence or appreciate how special God is in your life. Check the number indicating the intensity of your feelings. Let one equal the least likelihood of feeling God's presence, and five the most.

| 5 | 4 | 3 | 2 | 1 | | 5 | 4 | 3 | 2 | 1 |
|---|---|---|---|---|---|---|---|---|---|---|
| Alone in the midst of nature | | | | | | At Mass | | | | |

5   4   3   2   1
When with someone you
love in a special way

5   4   3   2   1
When with your family

5   4   3   2   1
When listening to beauti-
ful music

5   4   3   2   1
When sincerely praying
alone

As a class add other possible situations to this list and then discuss the following:

1. What difference does it make whether or not we personally experience the presence of God and his personal, daily love for us?

2. What are ways in which we can foster the awareness of God's presence?

3. What are ways in which we hinder it?

---

The material in this chapter is presented as follows:

1. God the Father as revealed to us by Jesus

2. God the Son as revealed to us by Jesus' actions and teachings about himself

3. The Trinity—the person of the Holy Spirit

4. The mission of the Holy Spirit to make us holy in calling us to be the brothers and sisters of Jesus

## GOD THE FATHER

In Chapter I we learned a great deal about God as he revealed himself to us in the Old Testament. And, as we saw, this Old Testament revelation is essentially the revelation of God, a loving creator of all things who calls his children into a covenant with himself. Jesus as God's divine son reveals to us yet deeper insights into the true nature of God as our loving Father. Understanding Jesus' teachings about the Father provides us with a vital key to appreciating God as Trinity as well as how God is present in our lives.

Perhaps Jesus gives us no more powerful an image of the Father than in the parable of the prodigal son (Lk 15:11-32). In this parable Jesus reveals that the love of the Father is radical, powerful, and beyond all human comprehension. The story presents the wayward son returning to the Father's house laden with guilt, and the Father rushing to meet him, not only forgiving him but bringing him back into the household to celebrate his return. The Father does not even see the son's sin but only his son, whom he loves without measure. The message of Jesus is that God the Father loves each and every one of us with just such a love.

In order to express this love Jesus called his Father *Abba* which, as we saw earlier, is a term similar to our term "daddy," denoting the most intimate and loving relationship possible between father and child. In many ways, Jesus' whole life and teaching center around the Father. He tells us that he came so that we might be united with the Father (Jn 17:20-26). We are to set the Father before us as the guiding norm of all our actions, striving to be perfect as he is perfect (Mt 5:48). We should forgive others the way the Father always forgives those who sin against him (Mt 6:14f, 18:35; Mk 11:25f). Jesus assures us that a bird does not fall from the sky, a hair does not fall from a head without the Father knowing it and being concerned and aware of the needs of all living things, especially of his children who seek him through faith in his Son Jesus (Mt 6:26-34). Jesus tells us as well that seeking the will of the Father is imperative if we hope to enter eternal life (Mt 7:21-23).

The Father also possesses the fullness of divine power. The Father alone knows the time when this earth shall end with the dawn of the Kingdom of God (Mt 24:36; Mk 13:32). The Father raises up Jesus (Rm 4:24). Jesus' whole life was a kind of sign pointing to the Father and his love for us. Even Jesus' last words upon the cross were words of abandonment to his and our loving Father, "Father, into your hands I commend my spirit" (Lk 23:46).

For Reflection and Discussion:

1. Have a scripture prayer service in the room by assigning each of the scripture references in the above section to a student in the class. (If the group is small, some will have to take more than one passage.) After the service allow for a short time of silent reflection. Then each student should write a paragraph on the aspect or aspects of God the Father that are the most meaningful or consoling to him or her.

2. What events in nature, our country, your local community or even your own life seem to you to be signs of the Father's loving care for us? Jesus went through severe trials and even death, yet never doubted the Father's love. What does this say about our own difficulties and our faith in the Father? What do the following texts say about this?:

> Mt 16:24-27
> Lk 12:1-12
> Jn 15:18-16:4

3. Saint Juliana of Norwich used to refer to God as "God Our Mother." Of course, God's love is in no way limited by what we understand by masculinity. In what ways do you think God's love has the qualities of a mother's love?

4. As a class read Lk 11:11-13. What does this text tell us about the comparison of our earthly father with God the Father?

5. The following prayer by Charles de Foucauld can be used as a prayer before class. What attitudes toward the Father do you find most appealing?

> Father,
>
> I abandon myself into your hands:
> do with me what you will.
> Whatever you may do, I thank you;
> I am ready for all, I accept all.
> Let only your will be done in me,
> and in all your creatures—
> I wish no more than this, O Lord.
>
> Into your hands I commend my soul;
> I offer it to you with all the love
>     of my heart,
> for I love you, Lord,
> and so need to give myself,
> to surrender myself into your hands,
> without reserve and with boundless
>     confidence,
>
> for you are my Father.

## GOD THE SON

The gospels relate to us how time and time again the disciples were perplexed by the words and actions of Jesus. They had left all things to follow him, yet they could not understand who he was or what he was trying to teach them. How can this be, they often asked themselves, that this man Jesus can calm the storm (Mk 5:35-41), heal the sick (Mt 8:1-17), forgive sins (Lk 7:36-50) and teach with divine authority (Mk 7:24-29)? Above all else, how is it that Jesus can raise the dead to life and claim that he himself is the source of eternal life for all who believe in him (Jn 11)?

The answer to the pressing question about the source of Jesus' power over evil, sickness and even death is found in Jesus' response to Philip who asked Jesus to reveal the Father to the disciples. Jesus' response is, "Whoever has seen me has seen the Father" (Jn 14:9). Coming from the lips of a devout Jew, that is, from one who deeply realized the utter sovereignty and glory of the one true God, this was truly a startling claim. And yet it expressed what the Christian community came to recognize as the very core and foundation of Jesus' identity; that is, Jesus is God himself who comes to bring us life through his life, death and resurrection.

As we saw above, Jesus taught that God is Abba, a loving Father who looks on us as his children. Jesus also states that with respect to his human existence he is perfectly like us and therefore in some way the Father is "greater" than he (Jn 14:28). But Jesus also claimed a unique relationship with the Father. Jesus tells his disciples that he was with the Father from all eternity before the creation of the world (Jn 17:5). All of his teachings are only what he received directly from the Father (Jn 14:24). He alone knows the Father (Mt 11:25-27). He says, quite simply, "I am in the Father and the Father is in me" (Jn 14:11). Thus, if we really know Jesus we will, at one and the same time, know the Father as well (Jn 14:7). What is more, it is by our becoming a disciple of Jesus that both Jesus and the Father will come and dwell within us (Jn 14:23).

After Pentecost the Christian community was able to realize that God was revealed to them not simply in Jesus' words about the Father. Rather, Jesus' very presence, his every word, his every touch, above all, his death and resurrection were in themselves actual revelations of God himself. Christian faith is founded upon the belief that "God so loved the world that he gave his only Son that whoever believes in him may not die but may have eternal life" (Jn 3:16). And so God is our loving Father. He manifests his love to us in creating us, so that we live forever as his children in his eternal Kingdom. When we fell in sin through Adam and Eve, God manifests himself to us as the Son, the one sent from the Father to save us from sin and death through his life, death and resurrection. Jesus is the God-man who comes to deliver us from bondage, to give us a share as the eternal Son of God (Jn 1:1-18).

*For Discussion:*

1. Use the texts cited above or any of the texts cited in Chapter II in a classroom scripture service on the theme of our lives in Christ.

2. Read Rm 5-8, 14. What does Paul tell us about our relationship to Jesus?

3. Boys Town of America has for years displayed a picture of a boy carrying a smaller boy on his back. The caption reads: "He ain't heavy. He's my brother." In what sense is Jesus our brother who carries us? How is our love for our brothers and sisters a model for our love for everyone everywhere? What parable of Jesus do you think brings this out most clearly?

## THE TRINITY

The above reflections on the Father and the Son as revealed in scripture enable us to examine the Father and Son as the first and second persons of the Trinity. This reflection will in turn provide the basis for our understanding of the Holy Spirit, the third person of the Trinity. As we turn our attention to the Church's formulation of its belief in the Trinity we must move from the time in which the gospels were written into the fourth century.

The first few centuries of the Church were marked by both bloody persecutions at the hands of the Romans and a phenomenal rate of growth in many areas surrounding the Mediterranean Sea. Literally thousands upon thousands of men and women made the free decision to risk death by becoming disciples of Christ and joining the community of the Church. This rapid growth produced a ferment of reflection on the gospels, and, in particular, on the identity and mission of Jesus.

In the context of this whole process a man named Arius (born 250 A.D.) began to promote in public the notion that the Son of God is not actually God but is rather only a creature of God. Thus, it is not God himself who became human, died on the cross and rose from the dead, but only a creature of God who was sent by God to win our salvation. Arius, in other words, did not question that Jesus was, indeed, both the word and the son of God. Arius did, however, say the Son of God is not himself God. Arius' ideas began to spread rapidly throughout the Church, causing much division and conflict among the people.

In response to this internal crisis, the bishops, under the leadership of Saint Athanasius, gathered together for the first major council of the Church, held in the year 325 in Nicaea, a town in Asia Minor. It was this Council, and some five others that followed it, that have given us the foundation of our present understanding of the Trinity as based on God's self-revelation given to us in scripture. The Councils (under the guidance of the Holy Spirit) took God's revelation of himself as Father, Son and Spirit and formed, through much prayer and reflection, a synthesis that succinctly expressed the Church's faith in God.

*The Father and the Son*

The Council at all times affirmed that God is one. God is pure, infinite, simple—a perfect unity. At no time is the Trinity to be understood as being three individuals, that is, three separate persons somehow looking at each other for all eternity. The persons of the Trinity are one. When one person of the Trinity acts, the other two act as well. They are truly distinct but never in any way separate. God is one. Sometimes an action of God is most aptly *appropriated* to one of the persons as, for example, when we say the Father creates, the Son redeems and the Holy Spirit sanctifies. But even here all three persons as one are fully present in each of these "missions" of the three divine persons. God loves us with one love and he knows us with one knowledge.

The Father is the person of the Trinity who is absolutely without origin. The Son proceeds from the Father. But here is where we must be careful or we fall into the same error made by Arius. The Son proceeds from the Father, but there was *never* a time when the Son did not proceed from the Father. Furthermore, the Son proceeds from the Father as the Father's perfect, divine knowledge of himself (thus the Son is called the wisdom of the Father). The Son is the Father's perfect, divine *expression* of himself (thus the Son is said to be the *Word* of the Father). The Father knows himself perfectly and this knowledge of himself is the person of the Son who is, from all eternity, fully, perfectly God. They are distinct persons yet they are in themselves, with the Holy Spirit, the perfect, simple unity of God.

## THE HOLY SPIRIT

It is at this point that we can introduce the person of the Holy Spirit. The Father and Son love each other with an eternal, perfect, divine love. This divine love the Father and Son have for each other is the Person of the Holy Spirit. The Son proceeds from the Father as the Father's perfect knowledge of himself. The Holy Spirit proceeds from both the Father and the Son as the perfect expression of their divine love for each other. Thus, the Holy Spirit is the Spirit of unity and love. The Holy Spirit is a Spirit that unites in love. As the Athanasian Creed expresses it:

> The Father is not made by anyone, nor created, nor begotten. The Son is from the Father alone, not made, not created, but begotten. The Holy Spirit is from the Father and the Son, not made, not created, not begotten, but proceeding. . . But the entire three Persons are co-eternal with one another and co-equal, so that, as has already been said above, both Trinity in Unity and Unity in Trinity are to be adored.

The Father
absolutely without origin

One
God:
Three divine
Persons

The Holy Spirit proceeding from Father and Son. The divine love of Father and Son. The Spirit of unity and love.

The Son begotten by the Father. Father's divine, eternal knowledge of himself. The Word, the wisdom of the Father.

We are able to know the Father and Son in and through their *missions* of creation and salvation whereby they become actively present in our lives. At this very moment the Father lovingly *creates* us and the Son offers us his healing, life-giving *redemption*. The same is true of the Holy Spirit. Through the revelation of scripture, we come to know the Holy Spirit as God in his indwelling presence which sanctifies us.

## THE HOLY SPIRIT IN THE OLD TESTAMENT

The Old Testament contains many and varied references to the Spirit of God. Jesus will use these veiled Old Testament images and build on them in order to reveal to us the Holy Spirit as a distinct divine person whom he will send into the hearts and minds of all who believe in him.

The opening lines of Genesis speak of the creation of the world, saying:

> In the beginning, when God created the heavens and the earth, the earth was a formless wasteland, and darkness covered the abyss, while a mighty wind swept over the waters. (Gn 1:1-2)

The reference to the Spirit in this text is not at all clear until one learns that the Hebrew word for wind is identical to the Hebrew word for Spirit. This explains why the *Jerusalem Bible* translation of the last line of this same verse reads, "and God's Spirit hovered over the water." The Spirit of God is thus associated with the *free movement of the wind,* with the *creative presence of God* and hence with *new life* and *new beginnings*.

Building on these same themes and giving them a yet deeper dimension, the second chapter of Genesis depicts God creating Adam by forming him from the clay of the earth. Then, Genesis says, God "blew into his nostrils the breath of life" (Gn 2:7). God's Spirit is here not only associated with a new life and a new birth but with Adam's own life which comes from God as God's own breath, that is, as a share in God's own life. Such images involving the Spirit of God appear often in the Old Testament (Gn 6:17, 7:15; Wis 15:11, 16:14).

The Old Testament also frequently associates the Spirit of God with the gift of *prophecy*. An Old Testament prophet was not so much a man who predicted the future as someone filled with the Spirit of God. In the Book of Numbers, for example, we find an interesting scene where Moses, filled with the Spirit, calls together seventy elders about his tent. The text reads, "The Lord then came down in the cloud and spoke to him. Taking some of the Spirit that was on Moses, he bestowed it on the seventy elders: and as the Spirit came to rest on them, they prophesied" (Nm 11:24-25; see also, 24:2; 1 Chr 12:11; Mi 3:8; Ez 2:2).

In similar fashion, the Spirit of the Lord was said to rest on the kings and judges of Israel. The Spirit lifted the leaders of the community above the ordinary ways of acting and thinking in the sense that the Spirit filled them with an inner light and strength to guide the people with *wisdom* (Jg 3:10, 11:29; Is 11:2). Most significantly of all, the Old Testament proclaimed that the coming of the Messiah would be a time when God would pour out his Spirit not simply on Adam or a prophet or a leader but upon all his people. This outpouring of the Spirit would amount to a kind of new creation, a new birth as the people would be filled in a new way with the living Spirit of God.

## THE HOLY SPIRIT IN THE NEW TESTAMENT

In the New Testament the Holy Spirit continues to be associated with new life and new beginnings. The Holy Spirit is the source of Elizabeth's conception of John the Baptist in her old age (Lk 1:15). And Mary, though a virgin, conceived Jesus in her womb through the power of the Holy Spirit (Lk 1:35). The Holy Spirit is again mentioned at Jesus' baptism by John. The scriptures tell us that,

> Immediately on coming up out of the water he saw
> the sky rent in two and the Spirit descending on him
> like a dove. Then a voice came from the heavens
> "You are my beloved Son. On you my favor rests."
> (Mk 1:10-11)

This text is not only significant in its mention of the Holy Spirit but also because it expressly refers to all three persons of the Trinity: Father, Son and Holy Spirit. No sooner does Jesus emerge from the waters of baptism than the Spirit leads Jesus into the desert where he is tempted by Satan (Lk 4:1). From the very beginning of Jesus' life we see that Jesus' whole existence was bound up with the action of the Spirit. He is a man led by the Spirit in all he says and does.

The message of the New Testament is, in part, that the Holy Spirit is no less active in the lives of Jesus' disciples. This point is forcefully made in the story of Pentecost as recorded in the second chapter of Acts:

> When the day of Pentecost came it found them
> gathered in one place. Suddenly from up in the sky
> there came a noise like a strong, driving wind which
> was heard all through the house where they were
> seated. Tongues as of fire appeared which parted
> and came to rest on each of them. All were filled
> with the Holy Spirit. They began to express them-
> selves in foreign tongues and make bold procla-
> mation as the Spirit prompted them.
> (Acts 2:1-4)

In order to really appreciate the change the Holy Spirit brought in the lives of the disciples we must recall who the Holy Spirit is in his divine life in the Trinity. The Holy Spirit is the eternal, divine expression of the divine love the Father and Son have for each other. The Father and Son are one in the unity of the Holy Spirit. *The Holy Spirit is then the Spirit of love and union between the Father and the Son.* When the disciples receive the Holy Spirit they are brought into a new union with the risen Jesus, and at the same time with the Father as well. This is precisely what Jesus himself told his disciples would take place upon his sending of the Spirit to them: "On that day you will know that I am in my Father and you in me, and I in you" (Jn 14:20).

Jesus is God's divine Son who is eternally one with the Father in the Holy Spirit. By sending the Holy Spirit at Pentecost the Father and Jesus make our source of union with them the same as their union with each other. Thus, the Spirit makes us the adopted children of the Father and brothers and sisters of Jesus. In the Holy Spirit the Father and Son are one in us and we are one in them! Paul tells us this, saying:

> All who are led by the Spirit of God are sons of God. You did not receive a spirit of slavery leading you back into fear, but a spirit of adoption through which we cry out, "Abba!" (that is, "Father"). The Spirit of God gives witness with our spirit that we are children of God.
>
> (Rm 8:14-16)

The Spirit gives the disciples *a new capacity to know and love Jesus.* By the indwelling of the Holy Spirit the disciples are no longer filled with fear but with a new courage born of the presence of the risen Jesus who is made present within them. By virtue of their reception of the Spirit the disciples share in the love and relationship that eternally binds the Father and Son together making them one. Thus, in the Spirit, disciples of Jesus can truly call God *Abba* for they are now God's children through the power of the Spirit which dwells within them. This reveals to us the fundamental meaning of the term *sanctifying grace* which God's own divine life made ours, through Christ's death and resurrection and the indwelling of the Holy Spirit. Truly, a Christian life, above all else, is a life lived "in the Spirit." It is, furthermore, a life lived in loving relationship with the three persons of the Trinity, with the Father our *creator,* the Son our *redeemer,* and the Spirit our *source of holiness* and God's *indwelling presence.*

For Activity and Discussion:

1. When God created the human family consisting of a
   father, mother and their children, he created a kind of
   image of himself as Trinity.

| The Trinity | Your Family |
|---|---|
| What is the origin of the Father? | How are the parents the origin of the children? |
| Of the Son? | What are the roles of the father in your family? |
| Of the Holy Spirit? | The mother? |
| What is the mission of the Father? | The children? |
| Of the Son? | What makes your family unique? |
| Of the Holy Spirit? | |

   a. How is love the binding force that makes the
      family one? How does this apply to the Trinity?

   b. Apply all of this to the understanding of Chris-
      tian family life as a life bound up with God
      who continually creates us, redeems us and
      dwells within us.

2. The triangle and the three-leaf clover have both served
   as traditional images of the Trinity. Discuss the reasons
   why you think this is so.

3. Compare the Pentecost story with the scene depicted in
   Ezekiel 37:1-14 where God raises up a mighty army
   from a field of dry bones. How does this compare with
   the experience of a deep conversion to Christ when a
   life apparently empty of hope or meaning is suddenly
   filled with new power and sense of purpose? Have
   you ever known anyone who had such an experience?

## Images of the Holy Spirit

The remainder of this chapter is devoted to developing further
the identity and mission of the Holy Spirit by means of a series of
meditations on the images of the Spirit given to us in the story of
the descent of the Holy Spirit at Pentecost.

### Wind

"Suddenly from up in the sky there came the sound
like a strong driving wind."

As we saw earlier the relationship between the wind and the Spirit goes back to the Old Testament. A divine wind was present at the creation of the universe. And God's breath brought life to Adam. It was a wind that parted the Red Sea so that the Israelites could cross over on their journey to the promised land (Ex 5:8). When the Israelites were starving in the desert, a wind brought quail for them to eat (Nm 11:31).

The Jews not only had an appreciation of the power of the wind to give life but also of the wind's freedom. Jesus himself stressed this point with Nicodemus saying,

> You hear the sound it makes
> but you do not know where it comes
>     from, or where it goes.
> So it is with everyone begotten of the
>     Spirit. (Jn 3:8)

---

Gather into small groups. Each group should then go through each of the following images related to the wind, specifying what the group feels the image suggests about the nature and mission of the Holy Spirit. Each group should feel free to add more images to the list.

A windmill that grinds wheat

A windmill that pumps water from deep beneath the ground

A cool breeze on a hot and pitch-dark night

Wind that brings rain clouds to parched land

Wind that sways huge trees

Winds that carry birds soaring in flight

A huge sailing ship being pulled through the water

Winds carrying seeds over great distances

A wind that makes a child's kite go high into the air.

---

At Easter Vigil the priest breathes on the newly blessed water. What is the significance of this? (See Gn 1:1) Relate this to the risen Jesus breathing on the disciples (Jn 20:20-23).

---

*Tongues of Fire*

The tongue, of course, is an organ of speech. We noted how in Genesis God spoke his "Let it be" over the chaos over which the Spirit hovered. We noted too how the prophets, filled with the Spirit, were able to speak with the words of God. Jesus, the God-man conceived by the Spirit and filled with the Spirit, spoke words of great power. His words calmed the storm, cast out demons, brought consolation to the lowly and even brought the dead back to life. At the Last Supper Jesus told the disciples that one work of the Spirit in them would be that of guiding them in their words (Jn 14:26, 16:13).

Reflection on the tower of Babel story in Genesis (Gn 11:1-9) throws further light on the significance of tongues as an image of the Holy Spirit. God brought an abrupt end to the construction of the tower of Babel by causing total confusion of the people's speech. Their inability to communicate was a sign that sin is the source of disunity and alienation between God and ourselves and between ourselves and one another. But here in Acts we note a kind of tower of Babel in reverse. The peoples of different languages are all able to understand the words of the disciples. This signifies once again that the Holy Spirit is a Spirit that *unites* all people to one another in a community of common love and understanding. Then the text in Acts goes on to relate the sermons the disciples gave about Jesus. The response to the disciples' words were mixed. Some responded with hostility, but others, many others, responded by becoming disciples of Christ. The Spirit had put power into the disciples' words. When they spoke, people's lives were changed. Above all, the disciples' words carried the power to open people's minds and hearts to accept Jesus into their lives.

---

Gather into groups and share with one another your insights into what the following images involving words tell you about the Holy Spirit. Again, do not hesitate to add images not in this list.

A word of friendship to one with whom we have had a misunderstanding

A word to a new student at school or to anyone who
feels isolated

A word of hope to the sick or the rejected

The words, "I love you"

A word of truth in a situation where someone or a
group is suffering some injustice

Words of prudent advice

The words of sincere prayer

Words of Gospel read at Mass

---

*Fire*

The tongues over the disciples' heads at Pentecost were tongues
of fire. Fire is mysterious; it is beautiful, yet it can cause great pain
and even death. In primitive societies it alone could light the dark
evening. It is the fire of the sun that made the crops grow. Fire
was then, understandably enough, an important Old Testament
image for the presence of God.

God himself was referred to as a consuming fire (Dt 4:24,
9:31; Is 33:14). God began his revelation of himself by appearing
to Moses in a burning bush (Ex 3:2). While on the Exodus the
Israelites were led through the desert at night by a pillar of fire
(Ex 13:21, 14:24). Exodus also relates how, when Moses was
receiving the Ten Commandments, Mount Sinai was "all wrapped
in smoke, for the Lord came down upon it in fire" (Ex 19:18).

The burning aspect of fire was used to symbolize God's judgment. Fire purified the holy (Is 6:6) but destroyed the wicked
(Gn 19:1-29).

As we turn to the New Testament we hear Jesus speaking of
his mission on earth by saying, "I have come to light a fire on the
earth. How I wish the blaze were ignited!" (Lk 12:49). Relating
the image of fire as the source of light we find Jesus saying of himself, "I am the light of the world" (Jn 9:15; see also, Jn 1:1-10).

Jesus applies the image of light not only to himself but to his disciples as well, saying, "You are the light of the world . . . you must let your light shine upon men" (Jn 5:14).

At Pentecost Jesus sent the Spirit who ignites the fire Jesus came to kindle. Jesus, the light of the world, becomes the disciples' own inner light. Their minds and hearts are illumined by the Spirit to know and love Jesus and to spread his love to others. They themselves become torches of light, living flames, going out into a world of darkness to spread the Good News of Christ.

---

Once again, you are asked to form into small groups. Share your reflections on the following images of fire and light. Again, do not hesitate to add images of your own, making sure you relate each to the Holy Spirit.

The fire of love

The fire in someone's eyes

Fire of a torch carried to light the way on a journey

Fire in a fireplace on a cold winter night

Fire at a lonely campsite

Fire of the sun which brings light, life and warmth to all living things

A fire in whose light we discover the presence of a friend

---

## Water

The image of water does not appear in the Pentecost story, but it is so central to other scriptural texts referring to the Holy Spirit that we will use it here to conclude our list.

Both creation accounts in Genesis (Gn 1-2) refer to water. The first refers to water in terms of a chaos out of which God creates (through the power of his Spirit hovering over the water) his world. The second account refers to God creating life from an arid desert. It is the water springing up in the arid wilderness that brings all

things to life. Thus, in the very beginning water has two aspects. First, it is a chaos, a swirling pool which God must tame in order to create. The second sense is that of water's life-giving quality in an arid land. In this latter aspect we find many references in which the Jews as a desert people compared water to God's presence, and their thirst for water with their desire for God:

> As the hind (deer) longs for running waters,
>   so my soul longs for you, O God.
> Athirst is my soul for God, the living God.
> (Ps 42: 1-3)

The chaotic, threatening aspect of water is brought out clearly in the story of Noah and his family (Gn 6-9) and also in the story of the crossing of the Red Sea. The Israelites waded safely through the separated water, but the Egyptians perished (see Pss 32:6, 69:3, 16). Here God is he who saved his children from the watery depths.

Jesus began his public life by his baptism in which he descended into the waters of the Jordan. As he rose up out of the water the Spirit descended upon him. He spoke to the woman at the well describing the gift of the life he came to offer in terms of water.

> But whoever drinks the water I give him
> will never be thirsty;
> no, the water I give
> shall become a fountain within him,
> leaping up to provide eternal life.
> (Jn 4: 14)

The relationship of Jesus to the chaotic, threatening aspects of water are brought out in the stories of Jesus calming the storm (Mk 4:35-41). But what is most significant here is that both aspects of water, that is, that of its life-giving qualities and its threatening qualities, are brought together in baptism.

Jesus tells Nicodemus that no one will enter the Kingdom of God unless they are "begotten of water and Spirit" (Jn 3:1-21).

An early Christian writer speaks of the waters of baptism as being both a womb and a tomb. The adult is immersed in the water as one who goes down into the grave with Christ, as one who dies with Christ. The new Christian's coming up out of the water is likened to Christ rising out of the tomb, victorious over death. Only if we die with Christ can we rise with him. This is brought out in the symbolism of Baptism. A baby is born from water in its mother's uterus. It is water that the first Christians found as the perfect symbol of new life in the Spirit. Thus Baptism became the *sign* that one was born again in Christ through the power of the Holy Spirit (Rom 6:4).

---

Again, form into groups. Share with the others the ways in which you think the following images help throw light on the mystery of the Holy Spirit. Add your own images involving water to the list.

Water in an oasis

A drink of cold water

A swim in the ocean on a hot day

Rainfall in the time of drought

A rope thrown to a drowning man

A bridge across a raging river

Water in the uterus

A powerful waterfall

Water in which fish live

A cool spring bubbling up out of the ground

Water sprinkled on dry seeds

A glass of water given to a thirsty stranger

---

## The Spirit Lives in the Prophets

A Christian prophet is a man or woman who is filled with the Holy Spirit. Such people provide us with the best possible way of observing how the Spirit works in our lives. Prophets move as the wind moves, bringing new and unexpected manifestations of Christ into the world. They are filled with the *fire* of God's love and often *speak* in ways that move others to change their lives for the better. Likewise, their Christlike kindness for others flows like a stream of fresh *water* into the arid deserts of hatred and indifference to the needs of others.

---

For Discussion:

1.  The list below consists of Christian men and women of present or recent times who are considered by many to be prophets.

2.  Members in the class can agree to research the life and teachings of one of those listed and then report their findings to the class.

| | |
|---|---|
| Mother Teresa of Calcutta | Thomas Merton |
| Jean Vanier | Catherine de Hueck Doherty |
| Dorothy Day | Pope John XXIII |
| Martin Luther King | Dom Helder Camara |
| Elizabeth Ann Seton | Cesar Chavez |
| Daniel Berrigan | Charles de Foucauld |

Looking back through history whom would you add to the list? Who do you feel does not belong on the list? Jesus once referred to Jerusalem as the city that "stones the prophets." Why will prophets always be the object of abuse and misunderstanding? What does the action of the prophet reveal to us about the action of the Spirit in the world?

2.  Every Christian is baptized a prophet, priest and king. What do you think it means to be a prophet as a young Catholic Christian living in today's society? In other words, what practices and attitudes in the nation, in the local community, at school or at home might call for you to take some kind of prophetic action? As a conclusion to this exercise all can share and compare their answers in an attempt to formulate a kind of class statement of what it means to be a Christian prophet.

---

## WHAT DOES THIS MEAN?

Of what importance is the Holy Spirit in the life of a young person? One approach to answering this important question is to ask another question—when and if you decide to get married, what difference does it make whether or not your spouse decides to live with you or to live 10,000 miles away? The answer, of course, is that to the extent your whole life is bound up with your spouse it will make *all* the difference whether or not you can live in the *presence* of your spouse.

So, too, we can say the Holy Spirit makes *all* the difference to the disciple of Jesus. The Spirit not only gives us the gift of faith by which we can know and love Jesus, the Spirit also makes the risen Jesus present within us. It is because of the indwelling Spirit that God can be said to be, as Saint Augustine put it, "closer to us than we are to ourselves." God is not merely in some far-off, remote heaven. Nor is he isolated in churches. Rather, he lives within us as his temples (1 Cor 6:19).

This can and should fill a young person with a sense of peace about the present as well as a sense of confidence about the future. Our feelings may change from day to day. Friends may come and go. But in the depths of our own hearts dwells the Spirit of love. A moment alone, a moment in silence need not be a moment of isolation, but can rather be a moment of sincere communion with the Spirit who dwells within us. Since the Spirit is the Spirit of love that unites the Father and Son, the indwelling Spirit unites us with others at a level that goes deeper than our weaknesses and blindness can destroy. Thus, even when we fail to understand one another, or fail to express our love to one another as we should, we know there is always hope of regaining and strengthening our bond with others because of the Spirit who dwells within us.

---

For Discussion:

Discuss the whole question of *presence* in general. Does the constant flow of talk—television, radio, records— keep us distracted to the extent we have lost touch with our own inner silence? Do you think that many people need to learn to be present to themselves, to listen to silence before they can learn to listen to God and to experience his presence within them? What are ways you think would help to recover this sense of presence?

---

OTHER QUESTIONS

*What Is the Catholic Charismatic Movement?*

Charismatic experience has been present, in many ways, throughout the long history of the Church. But the movement as it is today began in the spring of 1967. In February a group of about 20 people gathered at Duquesne University in Pittsburgh, Pennsylvania, to pray together, asking that the Holy Spirit enter into their lives with the same power with which he came to the disciples at Pentecost. The group experienced what they were convinced was the answer to their prayers. Above all, they felt a renewed and deepened awareness of the presence of the risen Jesus, and they were able to commit themselves to him in a way they were previously unable to do.

Shortly afterward a prayer group at the University of Notre Dame in Indiana, and other prayer groups throughout the world, began to experience the same kind of powerful, transforming experience of the Holy Spirit. Thus, experiences that previously were experienced by Catholics only in isolated situations now became a sweeping movement in the Church. Today there are literally tens of thousands of Catholic charismatics who claim that the movement is nothing less than a new Pentecost within the Church. The pope and numerous bishops praised the movement as being the work of the Spirit in the Church today, but have also urged caution.

Catholic charismatics are almost always associated with a prayer group or community which meets regularly for times of shared prayer. It is during these sessions of shared prayer that the phenomena associated with the movement most often occur. Sometimes the charismatics have an experience they call *baptism in the Spirit*. This does not refer to sacramental baptism but rather to an intense inner conversion of the person's whole life to becoming a disciple of Christ. The "baptism" may be a very quiet, almost unnoticeable event that is not recognized until days later, when the person realizes his or her renewed commitment to Christ. But sometimes the "baptism" is accompanied by strong emotional experiences.

*Speaking in tongues* is spoken of by St. Paul (1 Cor 13:1-3) and is reported as part of the experience at Pentecost. Speaking in tongues is fairly common at charismatic meetings. At any time during the meeting, one, several or many at the meeting may begin to speak in some language that the person himself or herself never studied. It has been verified, for example, that sometimes a person can begin to speak in Greek, Latin or some modern language such as French without ever having studied the language being spoken. Most often, however, the "language" is not recognizable as any known language. Often another member of the group will be able to interpret the prophecy or message to the group.

*Healing* is also a common occurrence at charismatic prayer sessions. Usually the healing is of an emotional nature or a situation in the person's life that is disturbing. The healing usually occurs when the members of the group "lay hands" on the person and pray for his or her recovery. Sometimes, however, the healing is of a physical disease.

Most charismatics would stress that these and other extraordinary signs are never to be emphasized in themselves. Rather, what matters is the individual's total change of life in order to become a disciple of the risen Jesus. Certainly, not all Catholics feel inclined to enter into such an expression of their Catholic faith. In fact, some Catholics are quick to criticize the movement, saying that a small minority of Catholic charismatics tend to compare themselves to others in such a way as to imply that those who are not charismatic are not as committed to Christ as they are. But regardless of one's personal feelings toward the movement, the fact remains that by it many Catholics have experienced a deepening of their faith in Christ.

## SUMMARY

1. In the Old Testament the Jews received God's self-revelation that he is the Father, Son and Spirit in veiled language that would not become clarified until the coming of Christ.

2. The early councils of the Church, under the guidance of the Holy Spirit, expressed this self-revelation of God in the theological synthesis we call the Trinity.

3. The persons of the Trinity are known to us in their missions. The mission of the Father is creation. The mission of the Son is redemption. The mission of the Holy Spirit is sanctification by dwelling within us, uniting us to the Father and the Son.

4. The images of tongues, fire, wind and water have a rich symbolic value in scripture and can help us understand the mission of the Holy Spirit.


## EVALUATION

1. The Jehovah's Witnesses claim to teach nothing but the Bible. Yet they emphatically deny that the Trinity has any foundation in scripture. Based on the material that has been given here construct a sound defense for the biblical basis for God as being Father, Son and Spirit.

2. In your own words, answer these two questions: Who is the person of the Holy Spirit in relation to the Father and the Son? What is the mission of the Holy Spirit, that is, what does the Spirit achieve in the lives of those who are called to be disciples of Christ?

3. In the light of what you have learned about the Father, Son and Holy Spirit, answer these questions which were first presented to you at the beginning of the first chapter of this book.

   a. Is there a God?
   b. If there is a God, how does he communicate with us?
   c. If he does communicate, what does he have to say?

## FURTHER ACTIVITIES

1. Read and reflect on the liturgy for Pentecost and also on the liturgical rites of Confirmation and Baptism. What do they tell you about the Holy Spirit?

2. The gifts of the Holy Spirit are wisdom, understanding, counsel, courage, knowledge, piety, and wonder (fear of the Lord). Look up the meaning of these gifts and report your findings to the class.

3. Have a charismatic Catholic visit the class or have a group from the class attend a charismatic prayer meeting.

4. Put together and celebrate a classroom liturgy on the theme of the Holy Spirit.

5. Read the Book of Acts.

6. The inspiration of the scripture and the guidance of the Church teaching are both attributed to the Holy Spirit. Research the meaning and importance of these two missions of the Spirit.

7. Have a group from the class interview a priest of an Eastern rite to have him explain the importance of the Holy Spirit in their theology and spirituality.

# 4

# The Christian Community (Church)

*And (I believe) in the one, holy, catholic and apostolic Church.*

(The Nicene Creed)

Did you ever notice your reaction to some very good news? Most probably, your reaction was the typical one of great impatience to share that good news with your friends and family. Because of our social nature we need other people with whom to share our good news as well as our bad news. We need the encouragement, support, acceptance, concern and love of others to make special events of our life meaningful and worthwhile. As the song lyrics so aptly put it, people who need people are the luckiest people in the world. This is so because, as the English poet John Donne wrote, "No man is an island."

We need others not only to survive but to become fully human. Infants need the concern and love of their parents. Children need the education and support which only others can provide. Young people need companionship and reassurance that only friends and concerned adults can give. Adults need each other and their children to provide not only basic services like police protection, food and clothing production, etc., which few individuals can personally provide in our complex society, but they also need a livelihood and a purpose to their lives.

Our need for human community does not stop with basic human needs. It also extends to all believers who need the love and support of others to sustain their faith. The Church is just such a support community. It is the community of people who believe in Jesus Christ. Jesus anticipated the basic need of a faith community to support, nourish and sustain his followers. In fact, he promised to send the Holy Spirit who would help complete his work.

> "When the Paraclete comes, the spirit of truth who comes from the Father—and whom I myself will send from the Father—he will bear witness on my behalf."                                            (Jn 15:26)

This promise was fulfilled after Jesus' victory over death, on Pentecost (Acts 2:1-4).

The founding of the Church on Pentecost Sunday shows that the Church is unlike any other human organization or community. Fraternities and sororities, for example, spring up on college campuses generally either to foster the social or intellectual growth of their members or to serve the wider college community. The Elks Club, labor unions, the Daughters of the American Revolution, even governments themselves are associations of men and/or women who work for a common purpose. All these organizations and others differ from the Church in that they were established by humans. The Church, on the other hand, is a unique organization, a one-of-a-kind community, because *it was established by God himself, in the person of Jesus.* There never has been or will there ever be a community like it. For this reason alone, it is worthy of our study.

This chapter will treat the following three questions about the Church:

1. What is the Church?
2. What does the Church do?
3. How do we recognize the Church?

But before we treat these topics, please pause here and reflect on a couple of exercises which will help introduce you to the topic of Church.

**EXERCISES:**

1. Please divide into groups of 5-6 students. Allow about
   15 minutes to try to reach a consensus (agreement) on
   the following points:

   a. What is the Church?

   b. Who belongs to the Church?

   c. What is the major purpose of the Church?

   d. If your group could send a delegation to Rome
      to advise the pope on what young people think
      the Church should be doing, list three issues the
      pope should address in the coming year.

Reassemble into a larger group. Share responses. Pick the
best definition of Church and compare/contrast it to what
you later read in this chapter. As a class, decide on the
three issues which you believe the pope should address.

Discuss:

   a. Why do you see these issues as so important?

   b. Do you know if any leader in the Church (pastor,
      bishop, pope, theologian) has already addressed
      these topics?

   c. Is there anything you as a young Christian can
      do to resolve these issues?

2. Your Church youth group has raised $3,000 this past
   year, by sponsoring some dances, car washes, a couple
   of raffles, and by soliciting donations from wealthy
   members of the parish. The group has decided to
   donate $1,000 to three separate causes. Below is a list
   of worthy causes the young people have come up with.
   First as an individual and then as a class decide which
   three of the seven listed here should get the money.

   Individual Choice                Class Choice
   1.                               1.
   2.                               2.
   3.                               3.

   a. The parish needs some money to send the pastor
      and his two assistants to a summer workshop en-
      titled "How to Give Better Homilies."

   b. An aged couple in the parish have just lost their
      home due to a fire. Their insurance covers only
      80% of the loss.

   c. The church organ is in bad need of some costly
      repairs.

   d. The parish gym, used by many of the youth for
      CYO games and dances, needs a new floor.

   e. The local bishop has appealed to the youth of the
      diocese to make some concrete sacrifice for the
      victims of an earthquake in Central America.

   f. The Education Commission of the parish council
      would like to have some funds to put out a little
      bulletin explaining Catholic faith to non-Catholics
      living in the neighborhood of the parish.

   g. The members of the St. Vincent de Paul Society
      would like to sponsor a meal once a week to feed
      the poor in an inner-city parish.

Discuss:

1. Should a youth group be concerned about any of these
   topics?

2. What criteria of selection made your class choose the
   three it did?

3. Would your parents have chosen any differently? your
   grandparents? If so, how could you explain the difference?

4. Can you think of any better uses of the money than the
   ones listed above?

---

Often enough, the problem in discussing the topic of Church
is the preconceptions people bring to the discussion. For example,
play a little word-association game with different Catholics. Ask
them to say the first thing that comes to mind when they hear the
word "Church." Are you surprised by the answers? Do people
tend to see the Church as a building? as people? as the body of
Christ? as laity? as clerics? as the pope? Of course, the Church is
all of these things, but some conceptions of the Church are more
important than others. The next section of the chapter will attempt
to clarify what Catholics mean when they say "Church."

## KEY TEACHINGS

Full authority has been given to me
both in heaven and on earth;
go, therefore, and make disciples of
    all the nations.
Baptize them in the name
    of the Father
    and of the Son,
    and of the Holy Spirit.
Teach them to carry out everything I
    have commanded you.
And know that I am with you always,
    until the end of the world!
             (Mt 28:18b-20)

Above all else, the Church is a mystery of God's incredible loving grace. The word *Church* translates the scriptural word *ekklesia* which means, literally, "those called apart." God, therefore, calls Christians apart to openly proclaim belief in our Lord Jesus Christ. The Church is the community of those who are called to acknowledge that Jesus is the Lord; it is a community of believers who live a sacramental life and who commit themselves to fellowship and service for the sake of the kingdom of God.

Because the Church is unlike any other human community, no one definition can precisely plumb the depth of its meaning. As a result, the bishops at the Second Vatican Council in the important document *Lumen Gentium* (*Dogmatic Constitution on the Church*) described the Church by the use of images. As a matter of fact, our leaders recognized that the Bible itself discussed important images of the Church which help us understand its meaning.

● **Church as Mystery.** To say that the Church is a mystery is not to say it is like some detective story which can be figured out if we but look for the right clues. Mystery is not used this way when talking about the Church. Rather, St. Augustine gives us a clue to the meaning of Church as mystery. He defines mystery as a visible sign of some invisible grace. Pope Paul VI sees Church in much the same way when he defines Church as "a reality imbued with the hidden presence of God." Therefore, to call the Church "a mystery" is to proclaim that the invisible, almighty God is present to his creation in and through a faith community who believe in and celebrate Jesus as the Lord.

• **Church, the People of God.** Perhaps the richest image of the Church taught by Vatican II is the Church as the People of God. This image has as its background the Old Testament covenant between Yahweh and Israel. God, who wished to make mankind holy and save them not merely as individuals, formed a single people. He taught them, preserved them and cherished them—all of this in preparation for the new people he would form in the blood of Jesus Christ who called forth both Jew and non-Jew (Gentile) to be united in the Holy Spirit.

The beauty and strength of this biblical image—People of God—is that it emphasizes the dignity of each individual Christian. As a matter of fact, the Greek word for people is *laos,* from which we get the word *laity.* Each Christian has been called by Christ into a fellowship of life, love and truth. As a fellowship, the People of God are used by Christ as an instrument for the redemption of all people, and are sent forth into the whole world as the light of the world and the salt of the earth. To truly belong to the Church and to be active in it means a person must help bring others to Christ both by example and direct effort.

Obviously, the Church (People of God) does not include all men and women. Rather, it includes those baptized members who proclaim that Jesus of Nazareth is the Lord (God) and the Christ (the Messiah). This proclamation allows the light of Christ to shine off on the world through them. By their words and most especially by their deeds, they draw others to the source of light and life, our Lord. They act as salt by adding a certain flavor to the world. Just as the presence of salt in food enhances its flavor and brings out the best taste, so, too, the presence of the People of God brings to the world and to other people the grand news that salvation has been achieved in Jesus Christ, that God's kingdom has been established in our midst.

This last point brings up an important question, namely, is the Church (the People of God) the same thing as the kingdom of God which it is to announce? In reality, the Church should be distinguished from the kingdom of God, that is, God's saving activity in human history which is drawing all people to him. The kingdom of God is broader than the Church. The Church includes only baptized Christians. The kingdom of God refers to all people who are to be saved, from Adam's time to the end of the world. But the Church and the kingdom of God are intimately related.

The Church is the initial budding forth of the kingdom of God, because its members work on behalf of the kingdom in an explicit, conscious way. The Church grows slowly, straining toward the fulfillment of the kingdom and desiring to be united in glory with her King. Also, because she ministers to the world in Christ's name, the Church advances the fulfillment of the kingdom in all persons of good will. The full flowering of the kingdom is the end product of all human history and it is the privileged task of all Christians to promote God's plan for all people everywhere and in all times.

• **Church: Body of Christ.** Perhaps the easiest image of the Church to preach is the image of the Church as the Body of Christ. The roots of this image reach the ministry of Jesus himself. He often identified himself with his followers, that is, with his Church. For example, to those who performed acts of love for his little ones, he proclaimed: "I assure you, as often as you did it for one of my least brothers, you did it for me" (Mt 25:40). He said to the disciples whom he sent to preach in his name: "He who hears you, hears me. He who rejects you, rejects me" (Lk 10:16). At the Last Supper, Jesus spoke of the oneness between himself and those who accept him in faith and love:

> I am the vine, you are the branches.
> He who lives in me and I in him,
> will produce abundantly,
> for apart from me you can do nothing.
>                                    (Jn 15:5)

Just as the vine and branches are one living reality, so it is with Christ and his Church, Christ and his loving brethren.

St. Paul is the one who developed the theme of Body of Christ in a sublime way. Undoubtedly, Paul was struck by the powerful question the risen Lord put to him when Paul was on his way to persecute Christians in Damascus: "Saul, Saul, why do you persecute me? . . . I am Jesus, the one you are persecuting . . ." (Acts 9:4-5). By persecuting Christians, Saul (Paul) had been persecuting the Lord himself. This insight given to Paul by Jesus prompted Paul to write to the Corinthian community: "You, then, are the body of Christ. Every one of you is a member of it" (1 Cor 12:27). The risen, glorified Lord is present in the world today through Christians. We are his hands, his loving touch, his understanding glance, his sympathetic word of comfort to the suffering and lonely, his instrument used to preach the good news of salvation and forgiveness.

Christ is the head of the body, we are its members. Christians become incorporated into the body through baptism. The principle of unity among the members of the body is the Holy Spirit for, as in the words of St. Paul, "It was in one spirit that all of us, whether Jew or Greek, slave or free, were baptized into one body. All of us have been given to drink of the one Spirit" (1 Cor 12:13). It can be said, then, that the Holy Spirit is the soul of the Church, a binding Spirit of unity who overcomes all natural divisions of race, color, nationality and sex.

The richness of the Church as body of Christ manifests itself when we compare this image to the natural human body. Just as in the body there are eyes and ears and feet and other bodily members which serve different functions, so, too, in the Church there are different roles to play. Some are apostles, some prophets, others teachers, and still others miracle workers, healers, assistants or administrators (1 Cor 12:28-31). The gift given to all, however, is also the greatest gift, and that is the capacity for divine Love. Reflect on these words of St. Paul, some of the most famous words ever written:

Now I will show you the way which surpasses all the others. If I speak with human tongues and angelic as well, but do not have love, I am a noisy gong, a clanging cymbal. If I have the gift of prophecy and, with full knowledge, comprehend all mysteries, if I have faith great enough to move mountains, but have not love, I am nothing. If I give everything I have to feed the poor and hand over my body to be burned, but have not love, I gain nothing.

Love is patient; love is kind. Love is not jealous, it does not put on airs, it is not snobbish. Love is never rude, it is not self-seeking, it is not prone to anger; neither does it brood over injuries. Love does not rejoice in what is wrong but rejoices with the truth. There is no limit to love's forbearance, to its trust, its hope, its power to endure.

Love never fails. . . . There are in the end three things that last: faith, hope, and love, and the greatest of these is love.

(1 Cor 13:1-8, 13)

The truth of the matter, however, is that at times the Church has failed to love. Because it is made up of a human dimension, as well as a divine, the Church can sin. And the Church has sinned in not being Christ. Our history as a Christian people does reveal that we are both holy and sinful. This is the paradox of Christian life: Christ comes to us through people like ourselves, people who are weak and sinful and not loving. We are a people on our way to total union with God. We are not perfect. God is not quite finished with us yet.

---

For Discussion and Reflection:

1. The variety of gifts by the Holy Spirit in the Church strengthens unity, it does not harm it. Can you see evidences of this in your parish community? Study your classmates. Select about five of them and note their real strengths, their real talents. How do these individual talents, perhaps all different, add to the larger group?

2. For various reasons, young people often feel alienated from the Church. However, if we take the Body of Christ imagery seriously, each member of the Church has something important to contribute, each member has some talent (gift) from the Holy Spirit. Can you identify your own gifts? How might they be used to build up the body of Christ in your home, your school, your parish, or your local community?

3. The people of God are both light and salt. As individuals or groups, perform some service for others which reflects these realities. For example:

    a. Collect food for the needy.

    b. Participate in pro-life days.

    c. Write letters to editors, legislators, T.V. stations and the like taking a Christian stand on some controversial issue. This takes risk; a person must be willing to suffer some criticism.

    d. Help old people in your neighborhood.

4. Read the following and make a brief report to the class:

    a. *Mystici Corporis*—the famous encyclical letter of Pope Pius XII on the Mystical Body of Christ.

    b. Chapter 2 of the *Dogmatic Constitution on the Church (Lumen Gentium)*—one of the most famous chapters in the documents which came from Vatican II. This chapter deals with the Church as "People of God."

    c. 1 Corinthians 12-13—these two outstanding chapters treat the Body of Christ imagery, gifts of the Spirit, and love.

5. Below are listed examples of some possible members of a parish community. Rank them in order of those who you think most build up the parish. Compare and contrast your list with those of your classmates. Then check to see what St. Paul has to say in 1 Cor 12-13.

    ———A wealthy widow makes a large donation of money ($50,000) to the St. Vincent de Paul Society. She enjoys the publicity she gets.

    ———A young teenage girl joins the choir because there is an appeal for members. She cannot sing too well but she wants to help out.

————The principal of the parish school, a layman, is very articulate in the local news media in arguing for aid to Catholic schools. He tends to alienate some non-Catholics and some parents whose children are enrolled in public schools.

————An old man faithfully attends Mass every morning. On some days, he is the only one there.

————A young couple has agreed to teach religion (CCD) in their home every week. They are quite nervous about teaching but they know the parish is in need of "host couples."

————A teenage boy coaches the grade school CYO basketball team. Their team record is 2-10.

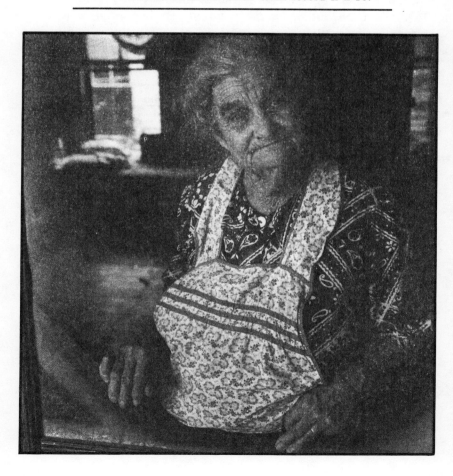

● **Church as Sacrament of Christ.** As we have already seen in Chapter 2, a sacrament is a special kind of sign or symbol. It differs from a traffic sign, for example, in its effect. A traffic stop sign points to the *idea* of "stopping"; the traffic sign does not cause (or effect) you to stop. It merely symbolizes through shape, color and words the *idea* of stopping. A sacrament, on the other hand, is an "efficacious symbol." It is something concrete that brings about what it points to. Thus, Jesus is God the Father's sacrament. He not only points to the reality of God, he is himself God. "Whoever has seen me has seen the Father" (Jn 14:9).

In a similar way, the Church is the sacrament of Christ. The Church Fathers at Vatican II put it this way in article 1 of the *Dogmatic Constitution on the Church:* "By her intimate relationship with Christ, the Church is a kind of sacrament or sign of intimate union with God, and of the unity of all mankind. She is also an instrument for the achievement of such unity."

What does this mean? Simply put, the Church is Christ's presence for mankind. It is an outward visible sign of God's loving gift of himself in human history.

Because the Church is a sign, like every other sign it must lead beyond itself, it must lead us to what it signifies, that is, to Christ, to God. The Church does this in three ways. *The first way is to proclaim the gospel news that the God of love summons all men and women to the fullness of life.* Some people have never heard this good news; others have only heard it in a partial or confused way. As a result, the Church must be a herald of the good news of God's love for us even within our human failings. The image of herald comes from the command of Jesus to the apostles on Easter Sunday in the upper room:

"As the Father has sent me,
so I send you" (Jn 20:21).

The heart of the good news is found in the *kerygma* of the proclamation of Jesus as Lord. The earliest form of the kerygma can be found in Peter's first sermon on Pentecost Sunday (Acts

2:14-41). There, Peter tells how Jesus fulfilled the Old Testament prophecies concerning the Messiah, how he performed miracles to show that God's kingdom has come, how he suffered, was put to death by Pontius Pilate, rose from the dead, and is now glorified with his Father. Peter concluded his sermon by asking people to turn from their sinful lives through repentance, to accept Jesus Christ in faith, and to be baptized with water in the Holy Spirit. The first task of the Church is to proclaim this good news of Jesus as Peter did.

*The second task is to build up the community of believers.* The Church does this by living the gospel it proclaims. If it did not, it would not be a believable symbol of Christ. To be an effective and credible sign of the gospel, others must be able to see the Church as a community united by faith, hope and love.

> "This is how all will know you for my disciples:
> your love for one another."
>
> (Jn 13:35)

If nonbelievers would see a loving, caring people, they would naturally have to take notice and ask themselves what does this group stand for. The technical term for this reality of Christian community is known as *koinonia,* or fellowship.

*The third task of the Church is known as "diakonia" (from which we get the word, deacon).* Diakonia means service. An image which describes this best is Servant. Jesus put it aptly at the Last Supper when he, the King of Kings, took off his cloak and washed the feet of his disciples. Footwashing was a menial task saved only for servants and slaves. But Jesus washed the feet of his disciples to show that to be great in the kingdom of God, a person must become a servant to others. *A Christian by definition should be a footwasher.* The name *Jesus* means savior/healer. Thus, a follower of Jesus must be a minister to the needs of others, a healer of their hurts. The Church must witness to God's love by translating it into acts of charity for all people, particularly those in need—the poor, the lonely, the imprisoned, the sick and the suffering (Mt

25:31-46). Actions speak louder than words. The Church which proclaims that God is a loving God who cares for people in their misery must be willing to take that proclamation and make it real by the deeds it performs for others.

In summary, then, the Church is a sacrament of Christ, his visible presence in the world when it performs three tasks: it heralds (announces) the good news of God's love; it builds up Christian community; it is Servant for all people, especially the "least of these."

*Other Images.* We have briefly discussed here the Church as mystery, People of God, Body of Christ, Sacrament, Herald and Servant. But there are many other images which describe the Church. Below are listed a few of these with an appropriate biblical quote:

- *Bride of Christ.* "Husbands, love your wives, as Christ loved the Church. He gave himself up for her to make her holy, purifying her in the bath of water by the power of the word" (Eph 5:25-26).

- *Mother.* "But the Jerusalem on high (the Church) is freeborn, and it is she who is our mother" (Gal 4:26).

- *Pilgrim.* "Beloved, you are strangers and in exile; hence I urge you not to indulge your carnal desires. By their nature they wage war on the soul" (1 Pt 2:11).

We will discuss the *institutional* aspect of the Church in the next section, "What Does the Church Do?"

---

For Discussion and Reflection:

For the Church to be a meaningful sacrament of Christ, individual Christians must be effective signs of Christ's presence both within the Christian community and for those outside the community. Discuss how each of the following can be an effective sign when performed by a young person in today's complex world.

- Mass attendance every Sunday

- Refusing to go along with the crowd

- Scripture reading on a regular basis

- Involvement in a service activity in the neighborhood

- Studying extra hard in preparation for one's future career

- Participating in sports in a clean, competitive way

Which of these would you say is most important? Why?

---

The Church Prays and Serves

Through class discussion, determine a specific hospital, senior citizen, orphanage, etc., which is in drastic need of food and/or clothing. Have each member of the class bring in food and/or clothing for the chosen person or cause.

At the same time, the class should carefully plan a classroom liturgy or prayer service. The readings selected might reflect the need to serve others as Jesus did. At the Offertory, food and clothes can be presented. Prayers of petition should be written for the recipients of the food. The class may wish to write a short sincere letter for the one(s) receiving the gifts.

After the experience is over, discuss the following:

1. Why is prayer an essential part of the life of the Church? In other words, why is the Church more than a social or charitable organization?

2. Why is service an essential part of the life of the Church?

3. Christ served others but constantly drew his strength from the Father. What does this tell us about the mutual dependency of prayer and service? How does all prayer draw us to action and all true action to our need for prayer?

4. In previous centuries, the Offertory donations consisted of food given to the poor. What was the significance of this practice? Should this custom be revived in churches today?

---

## WHAT DOES THE CHURCH DO?

We have already discussed somewhat the threefold mission of the Church when we treated the Church as herald, and saw its task to build community and serve people for Christ our Lord. This mission is briefly summarized as message, community and service. We emphasized there the individual Christian's duty to partake in this mission. Another way to discuss the mission of the Church is under the titles prophet, priest and king. Every Christian, we should stress, has a prophetic function, a priestly function and a kingly function. However, the Church as a whole in its institutional or organizational elements can act as prophet, priest and king. These three roles are roles which Jesus played for us and roles we as individuals and as an institution have an obligation to live. The emphasis in this section of the chapter will be on the institution, however.

1. *Church as prophet*. A prophet speaks the word of God. Every member of the Church shares in the prophetic mission of the Church. Parents, for example, have the duty and the privilege of sharing their faith with their children. Every member of the Church, by virtue of the dignity of being adopted as a child of the Father in baptism, is called by Jesus to witness to his truth to others. Once again, our deeds probably speak louder than our words, "In the same way, your light must shine before men so that they may see goodness in your acts and give praise to your heavenly Father" (Mt 5:16).

The Church has had many individuals who have stood out over the years to proclaim the word of God. These prophets have often been a shining light to non-Catholics. They have also called the Church as a whole to be true to its mission. For example, Francis of Assisi tried through example to show that the spirit of poverty brings men and women to God. St. Catherine of Siena witnessed loud and clear against the weakness of some of the leaders in the Church who were abusing their offices of leadership. In our own day, some recognize Mother Teresa as a prophet who awakens our spirits to see Christ in the poor and downtrodden. Or Dorothy

Day, the American pacifist, reminds us of our need to imitate the peacefulness of Jesus.

Not only do individuals in the Church have the gift of prophecy but so does the Church as an institution. Jesus entrusted to his Church the task of authentically and truthfully proclaiming the word as it appears in Scripture and in tradition. Authenticity and truth are preserved because Jesus formed a hierarchical Church. A *hierarchy* is a "sacred leadership." Christ chose to teach, to rule and to sanctify his Church through the bishops and pastors he appointed to care for it.

Catholic belief maintains that the successor of Peter, the pope, has a special role in the Church. In the center and at the head of the bishops, who succeed the apostles, the pope has primacy over the whole Church. We base that belief on Christ's own teaching:

> "Blest are you, Simon, son of John! No mere man has revealed this to you, but my heavenly Father. I for my part declare to you, you are 'Rock,' and on this rock I will build my church, and the jaws of death shall not prevail against it. I will entrust to you the keys of the kingdom of heaven. Whatever you declare bound on earth shall be bound in heaven; whatever you declare loosed on earth shall be loosed in heaven."
>
> (Mt 16:17-19)

Along with his fellow bishops, the pope and bishops form a single unity called the college of bishops. The bishops in communion with one another and with the pope have the task of teaching truthfully the word of God. They often do this when they come together in an ecumenical council, of which there have been 21. The pope's special role is to be, as it were, a sign or sacrament of unity of bishops who speak as one. As the Bishop of Rome, he has a special responsibility to be a living sign of unity in Christ for the universal Church. He is the head. He speaks with them as the voice of Christ alive in the Church.

Because of our Lord's promise in Matthew's gospel that the Church could not go astray from Jesus because of his continual presence, we believe that on essential matters of faith and morals, the Church is infallible. Infallibility refers to the belief that a certain doctrine (teaching) is free from error. The bishops as a group, of course in union with the pope, teach infallibly when teaching or protecting Christ's revelation concerning belief or morality. Although the individual bishops do not enjoy the prerogative of infallibility, they nevertheless can proclaim collectively Christ's doctrine infallibly. This is so, even when they are dispersed around the world, provided that while maintaining the bond of unity among themselves and with Peter's successor, and while teaching authentically on a matter of faith or morals, they concur in a single viewpoint as the one which must be held conclusively (*Lumen Gentium,* 25).

Furthermore, infallibility is expressed by the pope when he teaches "ex cathedra," that is, under the following conditions:

1. When he teaches as the visible head of the Church

2. To all Catholics

3. On a matter of faith and morals

4. Intending to use his full authority in an unchangeable decision.

(See *Lumen Gentium,* 25)

This kind of teaching is only rarely done by the pope. For example, only once in the last 100 years has the Holy Father proclaimed an infallible teaching, the doctrine of the Assumption of our Blessed Mother into heaven. Historically, papal infallibility has been very limited in usage. It refers only to the pope's power or gift as successor of Peter to correctly teach Christ's revelation to mankind. His personal beliefs and opinions, like any person's, can be wrong; for example, in politics, science, or sports. In addition, because he is human the pope can sin and make mistakes, even in the way he governs the Church. Like all gifts of the Holy Spirit, the gift of infallibility is not a personal gift to be gloated over, but it is given to build up the Body of Christ. It is not an imposition on our freedom, but an access to the truth of Christ.

Normally, the pope and bishops teach through the "ordinary magisterium" of the Church. The ordinary magisterium refers to encyclicals, pastoral letters, sermons and the like. Our general attitude to all teachings exercised by our leaders is one of respectful obedience.

2. *Church as priest*. The teaching office of the Church is important, but its purpose is to lead directly to the sanctification of others. Jesus came to make mankind holy, that is, make us one with his Father in friendship, to give us a life of love and holiness. He wished to form a priestly people so that all men and women could come in contact with the saving deeds of his passion, death, resurrection and glorification—deeds which redeem and make holy the entire universe.

Many activities of the Church lead to holiness. For example, the teaching and ruling authority of the Church has as its purpose the leading of people to the source of truth and holiness. But teaching and ruling do not exhaust all the sanctifying powers given by Christ. For example, Jesus instructed his disciples to baptize, to break bread in his name (celebrate the Eucharist), to forgive sins.

All Christians share in the common priesthood. As St. Peter puts it:

> You, however, are a "chosen race, a royal priesthood, a holy nation, a people he claims for his own to proclaim the glorious works" of the One who called you from darkness into his marvelous light. Once you were no people, but now you are God's people; once there was no mercy for you, but now you have found mercy.
>
> (1 Pt 2:9-10)

Just as some are called by Christ specifically to preserve the teaching of the Church, so there are some who have the specific call (vocation) and ability to make present the Eucharistic sacrifice and to forgive sin in our Lord's name. At ordination, priests are given the privileged task of becoming instruments used by Jesus Christ to confer his special sanctifying gifts. Special priesthood does not give personal honors for those ordained, nor does it mean that priests are necessarily better men. Though only some are called to be ordained to consecrate and to forgive sin, everyone in the Church is called to holiness—laity and clergy alike. The measure of our greatness is not the special gifts we have been given, but rather the intensity of love we have for God and others. At our baptism we have all been called to holiness, "to be perfect as the heavenly Father is perfect."

3. *Church as king.* All authority ultimately resides in Christ: "Full authority has been given to me both in heaven and on earth" (Mt 28:18). However, he has willed to share his authority with shepherds in the Church. As we have seen, he shares his teaching authority in a special way with the pope, bishops and pastors. He also shares his ruling authority in the same way and for the same reasons discussed above. The office of ruling has but one purpose, the growth of faith and holiness in the Church. Church law (especially Canon Law) and the legitimate commands of the pope and bishops are for the sake of the People of God and deserve respectful obedience.

Unlike so many kings and rulers of the world, the Church's role of ruling must be done with humility, love and compassion. Church standards must measure up to Christ our Lord, never to those of the world:

> Jesus then called them together and said: "You know how those who exercise authority among the Gentiles lord it over them; their great ones make their importance felt. It cannot be like that with you. Anyone among you who aspires to greatness must serve the rest, and whoever wants to rank first among you must serve the needs of all.
>
> (Mt 20:25-27)

The model of Church as king must be that of servant. The motto would read like this: "If you wish to lead, be a footwasher!" As a constant reminder of this truth, the pope has taken the motto "the servant of the servants of God."

---

For Reflection and Discussion:

This section of the chapter focused more exclusively on the "institutional" aspect of the Church. Many people today tend to distrust institutions. Even the Church has not been spared criticism. For example, some claim all the Church should do is "sell its riches and give everything to the poor." Notwithstanding valid points of criticism, consider the following:

    a. "The Church is the largest charitable organization in the world." Church-run schools, orphanages, hospitals, rest homes, homes for unwed mothers, and the like, the enormous sacrifices made by religious men and women and generous laity to staff these institutions, the need of a strong organization to keep these things running—all of these argue for an institutional aspect to the Church which sees that teaching, sanctification and service can take place.

        1. Make a list of as many Church-run organizations you can think of which operate in your diocese. Invite in some speakers from these organizations to discuss with the class how they fulfill the mission of the Church.

        2. Invite to class representatives from several different religious communities to explain what motivates their life-style and service.

    b. Study how the Lutheran, Presbyterian and Methodist churches are organized. Discuss the wisdom of having an authentic teacher (the pope) in matters of faith and morals such as we have in the Roman Catholic Church. Are there problems in not having a final arbiter?

    c. The ordinary teaching of the Church is conveyed through encyclicals, pastoral letters, sermons and the like. Read one of the following encyclicals and make a report on its teaching:

        Pope John XXIII's: *Mater et Magistra (Mother and Teacher)*
                                   *Pacem in Terris (Peace on Earth)*

Pope Paul VI's:    *Humanae Vitae (Of Human Life)*
*Populorum Progressio (On the Development of Peoples)*

---

## HOW DO WE RECOGNIZE THE CHURCH?

Traditionally, the Church has been known by four signs or marks which help identify its true nature. These signs are: *one, holy, catholic* (universal) and *apostolic*. The marks of the Church help to strengthen the faith of Christians and can attract the attention of the nonbeliever. But the signs are paradoxical in nature. They refer to the divine element (Christ and his Spirit) working in the Church. And, yet, the Church is made up of human members who at times seem to betray the very marks which point to Christ. We say the Church is holy and yet it is made up of sinners. We believe the Church is one, and yet there is a wounded unity among various Christian denominations. We claim the Church is for all mankind and yet individual Christians show prejudice to nonbelievers. Thus, these marks need some explanation.

1. *The Church Is One.* Unity is found in the Roman Catholic Church on three different levels.

> a. *Unity of creed (faith).* A creed is a body of beliefs. Examples of creeds are the Apostles' Creed and the Nicene Creed. The body of beliefs is officially put forth by the magisterium of the Church and all Catholics are united in their belief. The teaching of the Roman Catholic Church is unique among world religions in its clarity and completeness.

> b. *Unity of Moral Teaching (code).* The code of the Church refers to the moral teachings of the Church and their application to concrete contemporary problems. Catholics are united in the Church's continual quest to discover God's will in the solution to moral problems and are called upon to be guided by the moral directives of the Church.

c. *Unity of Worship (cult)*. The cult is the manner of Christian worship. The sacred liturgy, the Mass and the sacraments have unified Catholic worship through the centuries, as have particular forms of private prayer such as the rosary, devotion to the bible, and the like.

Unity does not necessarily mean uniformity, however. For example, there is unity in a family. Yet, the father's role is quite different from the mother's role. Even though Catholics from around the world believe the same truths, follow the same moral directives, and worship the same way, there is room for local custom. For example, the vernacular language in the Mass does not destroy unity—it is the same Mass. But the common language spoken in the region recognizes healthy differences between people and respects the rights of people to understand the Mass in their own language. But even though there may be differences from diocese to diocese around the world, all Catholics are united to the pope who is the symbol and servant of unity.

2. *The Church Is Holy*. The source of all holiness in the Church is its founder, Jesus Christ. The Church is holy because Jesus is holy and the Church is a special presence of Jesus. In the Church, too, are found the means of holiness, which can be defined as the "wholeness of personal development." God's will is that we develop as fully as possible as individuals. The Church possesses in a unique way the means necessary to achieve full personhood: the word of God which is found in the bible, in apostolic tradition, in the writings of great saints and theologians and in the teaching office of the Church; the liturgical life of the Church which includes the sacraments and most especially the Holy Eucharist; and in various kinds of prayer found throughout our Catholic tradition.

Calling the Church holy is especially paradoxical (an apparent contradiction) because of a sinful Church and the sinful lives of so many Christians throughout the centuries, even in the lives of some of our leaders. As a result, the Church is constantly striving for the holiness it frequently witnesses to imperfectly. Nevertheless, in every age countless numbers of Catholic men and women have led heroic (saintly, holy) lives of witness to Jesus and the Gospels. Often the times of the Church's greatest decline have seen the advent of some of its greatest saints, for example: Francis of Assisi, Catherine of Siena, and Ignatius of Loyola. Their lives add support to the belief that the Church has always offered the necessary means of holiness if people would but use them.

3. *The Church Is Catholic.* Literally, the word "catholic" means general or universal. The Church is universal on these accounts: first, following the Lord's mandate to teach all nations, the Church is available to all men and women at all times in all places. Poor and rich, learned and unlearned, men and women, all people everywhere are invited to be members of our Lord's body.

Second, the Church is catholic in the sense that it continues to teach all that Christ taught. The same essential faith and worship are held by a wide variety of people, separated geographically across the wide globe, culturally across the various races, and historically across almost 2,000 years. This is unique among world religions.

Third, catholic also refers to fullness. We believe that a Catholic has access to the fullness of a faith relationship to Jesus. This is especially true because of the availability of the sacraments, especially the Eucharist.

4. *The Church Is Apostolic.* Amazingly, the present leadership of the Church can trace itself back to the first leaders of the Church, the apostles. Christ founded his Church on the apostles who in turn appointed successors. Our present hierarchy is in direct succession to those apostles. The Church is also apostolic in the sense that it professes the same doctrine and Christian way of life taught by the apostles. It has preserved the good news of Jesus and has not changed anything essential in his preaching or that of his immediate disciples. The Church, in other words, is founded on, and continues the faith of the apostles.

Since apostolic times Catholics have venerated Mary the Mother of God as the perfect model of the Church and the Christian. Her role is unique among all Christians and among all women. She is the wonderful example of Christian faith, hope and love. As St. Augustine has said of Mary, she is indeed "clearly the mother of the members of Christ . . . since she cooperated out of love so that there might be born in the Church the faithful, who are members of Christ their Head." Thus, in many ways, she is the greatest saint and model of Christian life.

For example:

    a. She was the first and most genuine Christian. Her whole life was spent in an intimate relationship with her Son.

    b. She is our own example for Christian living. She continuously heard the word of God and kept it.

    c. She was attentive to Jesus, but this was not easy to do. (For example, read Lk 2:41-52 and Mk 3:34-35.)

    d. She was faithful to her Son, even to his death on the Cross. Her faithfulness was acknowledged by our Lord and by the early Christian community (Read Jn 19:26-27).

    e. She remains active as one who can intercede for us, just as she did at Cana for the young married couple (Jn 2:1-11).

    f. The Church is like Mary in that it looks to Christ continuously as the source of salvation; it looks to the world, entering into Christ's saving mission for all peoples; and the Church will finally see evil, sin and death wiped away (as in Mary's Assumption into heaven), and will have eternal happiness with God in heaven.

As a class, recite the Rosary. Carefully reflect on the mysteries and on the words of the "Hail Mary."

Write a brief sketch of a genuine Christian who would imitate Mary in the above points in the 70's and 80's.

## WHAT DOES THIS MEAN?

We have discussed in this chapter the founding of the Catholic Church by Jesus Christ. We have tried to present a definition of the Church along the lines of certain key images and then presented the mission of the Church and its distinguishing marks. It is time to pause here and ask how this all fits into the life of a young person. But before presenting a few observations addressing this question, please pause here and examine your own membership in the Church. Mark the scale at the point which honestly reflects your own feelings. Five means a very strong reason for belonging; one means a very weak reason for belonging.

I belong to the Catholic Church because:

1. I find Jesus there.

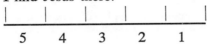

     5    4    3    2    1

2. My parents pretty much force me to belong.

     5    4    3    2    1

3. There is a sense of community, caring and fellowship in the Church.

     5    4    3    2    1

4. The sacraments, especially the Eucharist and the sacrament of reconciliation, greatly help me.

     5    4    3    2    1

5. I never really thought about it that much. I guess it is the thing to do.

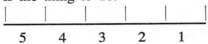

     5    4    3    2    1

6. It helps keep my beliefs in God alive and I suspect he wants me to belong.

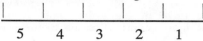

7. It is a good way to serve my fellow humans.

Did you ever meet a Mormon missionary? They are young people, usually 19 or so, who put in two years of missionary work to spread their faith. Or have you been awakened on a Saturday morning by a Jehovah's Witness who tries to convert you by citing bible quotes? Did you notice how young they were? Have you been surprised by their fervor, their zeal in spreading their religion? You may have been "turned off" by their religious faith, but perhaps you were impressed by their commitment.

Why do so many Catholic youth seem to lack the kind of enthusiasm for their Church that Mormon and Jehovah's Witness youth have? Do you suppose it is because we take our religion for granted? You may wish to discuss these questions in small groups.

In reality, though, we may realize it is a privilege to be a Catholic, that privilege does not make us better people. All people are equal in God's eyes, we are all his children. Rather, it is a privilege to know the good news of God's love for us and to be a member of his body which has the task of teaching and showing that love to others. Thus, this privilege brings a challenge, the challenge to be a prophetic, priestly and kingly people. In union with like-minded Christians, and in union with our Lord in the deepest way, most especially in the Holy Eucharist, we have the strength to live up to the challenge. We have the strength to be different because we have been especially chosen by our Lord to spread this word by the way we live. He told us, "I have chosen you, you have not chosen me." It is our individual task to use the gift we have been given and share the good news we are privileged to know.

For Discussion:

1. With your classmates, discuss the seven reasons listed above. Rank them in the order which you think should be the most important reason to the least important.

2. Give this same survey to three Catholics you respect the most. Discuss their answers with them and share your findings with the class.

3. Make a list of five things you personally can do in the next week that will show to you and others that being a Catholic makes a difference in your life. Post the list someplace to remind you to live up to your personal challenge to witness for Jesus and his message.

## OTHER QUESTIONS

Young people often ask the following question about the Church. Below is a brief answer to the question.

*Do you have to be a Christian in order to be saved?* This is an excellent question which people have been asking for centuries. Traditionally, the Church has provided the answer: "Outside of the Church, there is no salvation." This dictum, however, is very confusing and seems to be saying that non-Catholics cannot be saved. This saying does not mean that, although some Catholics have understood it that way. What does it mean? What it means is this: The Church is necessary for salvation because Christ is necessary for salvation. Jesus is the mediator between God and men; he is the one who saves: "There is no salvation in anyone else, for there is no other name in the whole world given to men by which we are to be saved" (Acts 4:12). Since the time of our Lord's ascension into heaven and his glorification with his Father, he is met on earth in an *explicit* way only through his Body, the Church. As people seek salvation, they will be drawn to Christ and membership in his Body.

In reality, though, many people have never heard of Christ. Others have only a distorted picture of him. Can they be saved? Yes. Those who through no fault of their own have not heard of

Christ are not beyond his saving grace. What is impossible for man is possible for God. Through God's mysterious plan, he wills the salvation of all people.

The kingdom of God does not exclude those who are mysteriously drawn to it through the workings of the Holy Spirit in their lives. If they remain open, loving people, then God's salvation touches them. Their task is to seek the kingdom of God as they know it. The Church is the *sign* in human history which points to the Savior, Jesus. (Read here especially paragraphs 14-16 of Chapter 2 of *Dogmatic Constitution on the Church.*)

However, a person who truly knows and understands the gospel should recognize the necessity of the Church for salvation: "He who hears you, hears me. He who rejects you, rejects me. And he who rejects me, rejects him who sent me" (Lk 10:16).

## SUMMARY

1. The Church was founded by Jesus, began on Pentecost Sunday with the giving of the Spirit, and recognized the need of human community with the risen Lord.

2. The Church is the community of those who are called to acknowledge that Jesus is the Lord; it is a community of believers who live a sacramental life and who commit themselves to fellowship and service for the sake of the kingdom of God.

3. Prominent images of the Church as mystery are: People of God, Body of Christ, Sacrament of Christ, Herald and Servant.

4. The task of the Church both in its institutional and human dimensions is threefold: the preaching of the gospel in truth (prophetic mission), the sanctifying of mankind (priestly mission), and service in love (kingly mission).

5. The Church is organized along hierarchical lines with the pope as Christ's representative. Infallibility refers to the special gift of preservation from error when teaching on faith and morals due to Christ's promise of always being with his Church until the end of time.

6. Mary is the perfect model for all Christians. Because she is the mother of Christ, she is the mother of the Church.

7. The Church is one in creed, code and cult; holy in its origins and its means of sanctification; catholic in its being for all men and women and teaching all of the gospel; apostolic in its line of succession and its apostolic teaching.

## EVALUATION

1. Once again, do the first exercise of the chapter. This time please do it alone.

2. In groups of five, write and illustrate an advertisement which should do two things:

   a. tell briefly what the Church is.

   b. encourage others to join.

### FURTHER ACTIVITIES:

1. Write an essay entitled, "What the Church means to me."

2. Read the life of your patron saint. Report on the significant facts of his or her life which have caused the Church to call that person holy.

3. Visit three churches in your area which are architecturally prominent. Look at the artistic representations in the churches. What do the buildings and art tell about the faith of the people?

4. Attend Mass at three different parishes. What was your experience? Likes or dislikes? What did that Eucharistic celebration tell you about the faith of that community?

**Your Class: The Living Church**

We have noted in this chapter that the Church is the active presence of Jesus Christ in the community. We hope that the following exercise will provide an opportunity for your group to experience your own place in the Church and in your community.

1.  Spend some time in small groups going over local newspapers to determine the most pressing social needs of the people in your community. Read not only the front page but also the business section, editorials, the social page, etc.

2.  In light of your research, list the three most critical issues from the perspective of making Christian ideals living realities in your community. These issues may be negative, for example, certain individuals or groups being treated in an unchristian manner, exploitation of workers, abuses of the environment. Or the issues can be positive, for example, groups or individuals fighting against great odds to bring about some gospel ideal.

3.  With the three issues determined and then expressed in concrete terms, find out the Church's position on the issue using both scriptural quotes and arguments from our tradition. Helps here might be the *Jerome Biblical Commentary, Dictionary of the Bible,* Catholic catechisms, this text and the *Documents from Vatican II* (with subject index).

4.  Using diocesan papers and interviews with local Church people, determine what is already being done in each of these areas. It is good to see, too, what other Christian denominations are doing as well as other non-religious groups.

5.  Finally, discuss what specific action the class could take, for example, a small donation, a letter to a councilman, a letter of encouragement to those who are involved, etc.

As this project develops, the following chart can be posted on the wall and filled in.

| The Specific Problems or Issues | The Church Teaching on the Matter | What Has Already Been Done and By Whom | What This Class Can Do |
|---|---|---|---|
| | | | |

# 5

# The Sacraments:
# Living Encounters with Christ

*Whatever was visible in Our Redeemer has passed over
into the Sacraments.*

(Saint Leo The Great)

As children, we learned that our world is filled with magic things. A tarnished old lamp contains an all-powerful genie. A secret ring, found in a trunk in Grandma's attic can grant us any three wishes. A moth-eaten old cloak will let us wander through the world unseen by human eyes. A magic wand (in the hands of a kind old fairy godmother) can transform a peasant girl into a dazzling young princess. As children, we looked at ordinary things and saw beyond them to a wonderful world of mystery.

This chapter is about the seven sacraments. And in order to appreciate the sacraments we must, while growing into adulthood, retain the simplicity of children. We must retain the ability to look at life and, in faith, see a deeper dimension to it. But unlike the magic of childhood fantasies, the sacraments are holy events, holy moments in which Christ touches us in the simple realities of everyday life. Our faith gives us the ability to recognize the living Jesus in the bread and wine of the Eucharist. Our faith allows us to discover that the water used in baptism is charged with the power of the Spirit, and the words of the priest in the sacrament of reconciliation are the words of Jesus telling us that we are healed and restored to union with God.

113

In this chapter we will discuss the sacraments under the following headings:

1. The meaning of the terms *sign, symbol* and *sacrament.*

2. Jesus and the Church as sacraments.

3. The seven sacraments considered as Christ touching us in the key moments of our lives.

---

**Looking at our present understanding of the sacraments**

In order to begin reflecting on the sacraments you are asked to do the following exercise intended to help you become aware of your present knowledge of the sacraments:

Gather into small groups. Each group should determine what it thinks is the most important thing to know about each of the sacraments. After allowing time for all to finish, the groups can share their answers with the rest of the class.

Baptism _____

Confirmation_____

Reconciliation_____

Anointing of the Sick_____

Marriage _____

Ordination_____

Eucharist_____

---

## SIGNS AND SYMBOLS

Before going on to discuss the sacraments as such we must first pause to appreciate the meaning of the terms sign and symbol and what it means to say the sacraments are a very special kind of symbol in which we meet Christ.

A sign is anything that suggests the existence of some other reality which is not readily evident. For example, a flashing red light and a clanging bell at a railroad crossing are signs a train is coming. A lump on a woman's breast is a sign of a tumor or possible cancer. A barber pole in front of a store is a sign there is a barber shop within.

It is important to understand that these signs only *suggest* the existence of the train, the tumor or the barber shop; these things do not necessarily have to be there. The tumor may not exist, the railroad gate could be stuck causing the alarms to go off, and the barber pole could be standing in front of a long-empty building.

---

What are some other signs, that is, other things which point to or indicate some other unseen, unheard reality? Why is it important to learn to "read" such signs? How is a spoken word a sign?

---

A symbol is also a sign, but a much richer sign, one containing greater depth of meaning. Both have this in common: they have a dual nature—their own reality and the outside reality they point to.

Rather than *suggesting* something outside itself, the symbol offers meaning within itself associated with the outside reality. In that sense it contains that which it signifies.

For example, a ring which has no beginning or end, becomes the spouses' gift to each other in marriage, signifying the unbrokenness (fidelity) and eternity of their love. The couple looks at their rings and sees more than a gold circle. They see in the ring their pledge of developing love and fidelity. The symbol contains that which it signifies and helps sustain what it signifies.

Another example that might help is the American flag. The very design of the flag is a sign of the unity of the States and their beginnings in the first colonies. However the flag is also a symbol. We have strong images of the tattered flag still flying after a night of bombardment at Ft. McHenry (hence the words to the "Star-Spangled Banner"), Betsy Ross sewing the banner for colonial troops, or the Marines placing the flag on Iwo Jima.

Think of how offended people are when the flag is burned or trampled by demonstrators. It is not enough to dismiss the action by saying "it's just a piece of cloth," because the piece of cloth contains a much deeper meaning. For one, it represents the nation's victories over adversity. In this sense the symbol contains what it signifies. The flag also brings about what it signifies in the sense that its very existence stimulates our feelings of patriotism, feelings which help the nation overcome adversity.

## THE SYMBOLS OF GOD

As we saw in chapter one, God is both immanent and transcendent, that is, God is both utterly within, yet utterly beyond his creation. When he speaks to us through his presence in his creatures, he does not do so in the obvious, more superficial manner of signs but rather in the deeper yet more mysterious manner of symbols. He does not, for example, speak to us on the evening news or write messages to us on billboards. Rather, he mysteriously speaks to us in the beauties of nature or in the gift of a friend. He is present in all the things he has made. Saint Francis of Assisi is said to have been so sensitive to the presence of God in the simple realities of life that he referred to fire as "brother fire" and to water as "sister water." Fire and water were to him alive with God's presence. They were symbols that somehow allowed him to glimpse the presence of God dwelling within them.

---

**Activity:**

The following is a list of symbols which can be interpreted as conveying profound meaning. From this list, choose three (or add some) which deeply help you to sense the presence of God. Choose three which are not too helpful. Give reasons for your choices.

a. A sunset over a body of water
b. The birth of a baby
c. A kiss between two lovers
d. A violent thunderstorm
e. A handshake between friends
f. A warm fire on a cold night
g. Children laughing and playing
h. Sharing food with someone
i. Healing a wound
j. A word of forgiveness
k. A field of wild flowers
l. A star-filled night

1. *Helpful symbols:*

    a._____is a helpful symbol because
    _____.

    b._____is a helpful symbol because
    _____.

    c._____is a helpful symbol because
    _____.

2. *Symbols which are not too helpful:*

    a._____is not too helpful because
    _____.

    b._____is not too helpful because
    _____.

    c._____is not too helpful because
    _____.

## THE CONDITIONS NECESSARY FOR OUR BECOMING AWARE OF SYMBOLS

Signs are superficial and obvious. Symbols are deep and mysterious. In fact, we can sometimes miss entirely the symbols of life. We can fail to "hear" love in the voice of a friend or to "see" the need to be noticed in the face of a child. We can miss the symbols of God as well. We can fail to "see" God in children at play or to "hear" him in the song of a bird. If we are open to symbols our lives are rich and full. Without symbols our lives quickly become sterile and empty. We might then easily ask ourselves the conditions or circumstances that allow us to encounter the inner, spiritual realities of life in and through the simple, concrete realities that fill our everyday lives. Listed below are some guidelines that can help us be more conscious of what enables us to be aware of symbols:

1. A symbol calls for *faith*. It is physical, yet it points beyond itself. The symbol can become meaningful only in an act of faith in what is hidden from our senses. The two people in love will never see each other's love. They will see only its symbols in which they will constantly believe.

2. The symbol brings about an active encounter between ourselves and God or between ourselves and another. The symbol is not an inanimate object or an empty ritual. The gift of a rose, a sincere word of concern are moments, words, objects, actions that are filled with meaning that bring about a deeper union of love.

3. Because of this, the symbol must be received actively. There must be the proper attitudes and the genuine desire to find in the symbol the love it signifies. Otherwise, symbols can be missed. We can lose our ability to enter into the symbol and then the relationship being symbolized becomes cold and can possibly die.

4. The symbol actually contains and brings about what it signifies. The man does not say to his wife, "This embrace is a representation of my love." Rather, the two know that the embrace itself somehow makes their love available to them. This is true not only with human symbols but with divine symbols as well. God remains transcendent, that is, infinitely above his creation, yet he is intimately present in his creation. The warmth of the sun should be for us a way of feeling the warmth of his love. And a soft summer rain should allow us to feel and hear his gentle concern for our needs.

---

For Discussion:

Jesus once said, "You have eyes to see but do not see and ears to hear but do not hear." Apply this statement of Jesus to the points made above about symbols.

---

## JESUS—THE PERFECT SACRAMENT OF GOD

The term sacrament refers to a very special kind of symbol in which God himself can be found and worshipped. This is not true of the symbols of God in nature. God is truly present in a tree and we should be able to see something of God's beauty present there. But we should not worship the tree, for although God is truly immanent (present) within the tree, he is also transcendent.

But in a sacrament this is not the case. A sacrament is a symbol in which God himself is actually, actively present. Thus, *Jesus is the perfect sacrament of God.* Jesus is the God-Man. He is at once human (thus seeable and hearable) yet truly divine and thus worthy of our worship. Jesus is God whose words we can hear with our ears and whose touch we can feel with our skin. When Jesus embraced a child it was God's embrace. When Jesus cured the infirm it was God's healing power at work.

---

For Reflection:

1. Complete the following in your own words:

   As seeing fire is seeing light, as holding the hand of a loved one is a way of holding love, so too, seeing Jesus is seeing God because ............................................

2. As a class reflect for a moment on the gospels. Who *actually saw* Jesus? Who *actually heard* him? Use the guidelines just given in the "conditions necessary for becoming aware of symbols" in arriving at your answers.

---

## THE CHURCH—THE PERFECT SACRAMENT OF JESUS

It would seem that Jesus' ascension into heaven marked the end of his being our sacrament, our living encounter with God. Once he went away he was, one might imagine, no longer with us as the touchable, hearable, seeable God present in our midst.

Yet we know that such is not the case. At Pentecost Jesus poured the Spirit into the hearts of his disciples, making them into the physical-spiritual symbol of his resurrected presence. The Spirit not only enlightened their minds enabling them to recognize the Lordship of Jesus; the Spirit also transformed them from within, making them into a new creation in Christ. They themselves became the living symbol that actually contained and made present the risen Jesus in the world around them. And it is in this way that the risen Jesus remains present on earth today. The fathers of the Second Vatican Council state that as Jesus the God-Man made God present in the world as a living, visible symbol of God's presence, so too the Church, as the Spirit-filled community, is the living symbol of the risen Jesus living in the world today. The council fathers write in *The Constitution on the Church:*

> It (the Church) is compared to the mystery of the Incarnate Word. As the assumed nature inseparably united to the divine word serves him as a living organ of salvation, so, in a similar way, does the visible social structure of the Church serve the Spirit of Christ, who vivifies it, in the building up of the body.
>
> (cf Eph 4:16) No. 8

Through the sacrament of the Church, Jesus is present in the world. We who possess the Spirit, we the disciples of Jesus are called to be Church, that is, to be Christ's voice and Christ's hands in the world around us.

---

For Reflection:

1. What does it mean to say that if others are to meet Jesus they must meet him in us? What does it mean to be a living sacrament of Jesus in the world around us?

2. Have you ever met someone whom you admired very much and who was a genuinely committed Christian? Do you think the world today needs more people like this? What stops each of us from striving to become such a person ourselves?

## THE SEVEN SACRAMENTS

The words and actions, the life and death of Jesus signify God's redemptive love for and identification with his children. And Jesus not only signified our salvation but he also, in his very person, brought about the redemption he signified. In this way a sacrament brings about what it signifies and signifies what it brings about.

The Church, as noted previously, is the sacrament of Jesus. The Church signifies that Jesus continues to live in the world through the presence of the community which believes in him as Lord. It also means that the presence of the Church not only signifies (symbolizes) the presence of Jesus, but also causes this presence.

Thus when a Christian serves the poor in the name of Christ, it is actually Christ, in and through his disciples, who continues to touch and console the poor. So, too, when the community of the Church gathers for the celebration of the Eucharist, it is actually Jesus in his Spirit-filled community who offers himself to the Father.

Jesus is always present in the community of the Church but the seven sacraments are given to us by Christ in order that we may realize how he is present to us. Christ touches us in the core of our lives. He touches us in the critically important and decisive moments of our lives. He transforms those moments into living encounters with him. *The central, vital moments of our lives as touched by Christ are called sacraments.*

In each of the seven sacraments, Christ's presence is signified in some way. There are some spoken words so that his presence can be heard. There are visual elements such as bread and wine, water or oil so that his presence can be seen and felt.

For example, at baptism, in the words spoken by the priest, parents and witnesses, in the water poured over the baby's head, Christ acts in a real, tangible, hearable way by touching the mystery of new life. Thus, the baptism not only signifies New Life in Christ, it actually brings it about. It makes the New Life in Christ a living reality in the newborn infant. We must, of course, always respond freely to Christ present in his sacraments. Our failure to respond cannot lessen or remove his presence there but it can greatly lessen or hinder altogether the ability of his presence to change our lives.

---

Go back to page 118 to the list of guidelines for helping us be aware of symbols. Apply each of these guidelines to our presence at the sacraments.

---

With this understanding of sacraments as sacred encounters with Christ active in the key moments of our lives, we can now turn to a brief look at each of the seven sacraments. But before we do this we will take a brief look at what are called the sacramentals.

## THE SACRAMENTALS

The sacramentals are all those things and actions which help us become more aware of Christ's presence in our lives. A study of the sacramentals can help us to appreciate better an important aspect of our Roman Catholic tradition of Christianity.

---

**A Look at the Sacramentals of the Church**

Listed below are a number of the sacramentals of the Church. For the sake of clarity, they are divided into several main categories. As a class, you are asked to share what you know about each and what each signifies about our relationship with Christ. For example, candles represent Christ the Light.

After the sharing is over: 1. Discuss the elements in contemporary society that make it difficult for us today to relate authentically to and benefit from some of the traditional sacramentals of the Church, and 2. Discuss what might be some contemporary sacramentals for today's Christians.

## OBJECTS

| | | | |
|---|---|---|---|
| candles | incense | church | priest's |
| holy water | relics | buildings | vestments |
| icons, statues | pictures | rosary | |

## ACTIONS

| | | | |
|---|---|---|---|
| sign of the | kneeling | sign of peace | extending hands |
| cross | bowing the | at Mass | palm up to |
| genuflecting | head | saying prayers | receive Euchar- |
| | | singing hymns | ist |

## PLACES

| | | |
|---|---|---|
| Holy Land | Lourdes | Guadalupe |
| Rome | Fatima | Shrine of Saint |
| | | Ann de Beaupre |

Morning and evening prayer

Early Christians would sometimes gather and pray in common at morning and evening. This practice developed into the canonical office which for centuries was sung or recited by most religious orders and diocesan priests. Today, many parishes continue this practice in communal evening prayer or Vespers.

Fasting

Fasting is an ancient and important Christian practice which symbolizes the Christians' share in the cross of Christ.

Sacred time

Besides the importance of sacred places such as the Holy Land there is also sacred time which refers to the liturgical seasons of the year. In Advent, for example, the sincere Christian is asked to enter into a spiritual preparation for the coming of Christ.

## THE SACRAMENTS OF INITIATION:
## BAPTISM, CONFIRMATION, EUCHARIST

As noted above, in the seven sacraments Jesus touches us in the most vital moments of our lives. All life, of course, begins with birth. And *Baptism* is the sacrament of our reception of the Holy Spirit who grants us new, eternal life by allowing us to share in the resurrected life of Jesus.

In the early Church, the sacrament of Baptism was administered along with the sacraments of Confirmation and the Eucharist. All three were considered sacraments of initiation into the believing community. Here we will reflect on each of these three sacraments as they were administered in the early Church and then relate each to our daily Christian life.

## BAPTISM

In the early Church preparation for baptism took months and often years of prayerful, careful reflection. Baptism meant a total commitment to Christ. No one who was indifferent or only half-committed was accepted for baptism. This was especially so during the times of the persecutions by the Romans when belonging to the Church could literally involve dying in witness to Christ.

Baptism was administered on Holy Saturday Night, and the weeks of Lent preceding baptism were spent in fasting, study of the faith and prayer. Finally, on Holy Saturday Night, those to be baptized (called *catechumens*) joined the believing community for the first part of the Eucharistic liturgy.

At the end of the readings those already baptized stayed in church to pray for those to be baptized as they were led from the church to a nearby baptismal pool. There the men were separated from the women. Those to be baptized removed their clothing as a sign of their being stripped of all attachment to sin and worldly pleasures. Then the men led by a man and the women led by a woman were taken one by one into the baptismal pool where they were each briefly and gently immersed three times beneath the surface of the water. This immersion was a powerful sacramental that the one baptized was now dead to the old self of sin. Descending into the water like Christ descending into the tomb, he/she vanished from sight only to rise a moment later from the water like Christ risen from the tomb. And, as they rose, they heard the words of Christ through the one baptizing them, "I baptize you in the name of the Father, the Son and the Holy Spirit." After baptism, each was led from the pool and immediately clothed in a white robe, signifying their new life in Christ. Finally, there were some concluding prayers and the anointing with oil.

## CONFIRMATION

Confirmation recalls the descent of the Holy Spirit on the disciples at Pentecost. Before the descent of the Spirit the disciples were afraid and without faith. But the Spirit totally transformed them into courageous, outspoken, fully convinced disciples of Christ. In the early Church, confirmation followed baptism as a sign of strength and the full commitment implied in baptism.

The one confirmed was anointed with chrism (an oil made of a mixture of olive oil and balsam) and received the laying on of hands accompanied by the words of confirmation. In biblical times, oil was an important symbol of strengthening, and also of special consecration such as for priests and kings. Oil in confirmation symbolizes our strengthening by the Holy Spirit, and our being consecrated by the Spirit as God's holy people.

## EUCHARIST

Later on, a whole chapter will be devoted exclusively to the topic of the Eucharist. Here we will refer to the Eucharist briefly as part of the early Church's initiation into the believing community.

The reception of the Eucharist immediately followed the rite of confirmation. This first reception of the Eucharist on the night of baptism provided a powerful symbol that it is the risen Jesus whose resurrected life is given to us. It is the same risen Jesus who continues to nourish us on our daily journey from new birth in baptism to the Father's kingdom. A baby is born once but is nourished often. So, too, baptism and confirmation are received once, but the Eucharist, our heavenly nourishment, is received throughout Christian life.

---

Activities and Discussion:

1. Imagine you are a young, newly baptized Christian of the early Church. In fact, it is Easter Sunday and you were baptized, confirmed and received first Eucharist only hours ago. Your decision to follow Christ has changed your whole life. You know at times it will be difficult to be a true disciple of Christ. You may even have to undergo martyrdom rather than deny Christ. But still you are filled with deep peace and joy. And now you are sitting down to write an epistle to your best friend in a distant town to tell him about your new life in Christ.

   As a brief assignment, write this letter. Include what you think would actually be your deepest concerns and sentiments.

2. The early Church reserved baptism primarily for adults, emphasizing that being a Christian involves a free, adult decision to be a follower of Christ. Today, the Church primarily baptizes infants, emphasizing the need for the Christian family to gradually nurture attitudes of faith during childhood in preparation for an eventual, hoped-for free acceptance of Christ as an adult. As a class, discuss the possible advantages and disadvantages of both adult and infant baptism.

3. The sacrament of confirmation is a sacrament of initation. Yet over the centuries this sacrament gradually became reserved for later years. Some today say the sacrament should once again be made part of the baptismal rite. Still others point out the need for a sacramental expression of the adult decision to follow Christ. These people urge that confirmation be made optional and be reserved to senior high school or later. Discuss the strengths and weaknesses of both these positions.

4. Discuss the present liturgy for Holy Saturday night. What elements of the early Church liturgy can you recognize?

---

## MARRIAGE

A baby is born and is nourished and strengthened through the years of childhood and finally becomes a young adult. Then, most often, the young man or woman enters into marriage. Few things in life affect us as extensively and as deeply as does marriage. In marriage spouses share all joys and sorrows, all successes and failures, and even their bodies in an intimate way. In the loving union of marriage, children are brought into the world. And the children with their parents form the family which is the foundation of human society.

The Church's celebration of marriage as a sacrament is an expression of its realization that in marriage Jesus touches the very core of our lives.

Marriage is a fundamental way to journey with Christ to the Father. It is a sacrament not just in the moment of the rite of marriage, but rather remains a sacrament all through the couple's life.

In fact, in marriage, the Christian couple expresses their faith two ways: First, Jesus' love for them is the model of their love for each other. The power of the risen Jesus is the power which will sustain them in all their hardships as well as enrich them in all their happy moments. Second, the couple expresses in a Christian marriage that they are called to be living sacraments of Christ's love to each other. In their mutual words of encouragement and embraces of love they will hear and touch the words and embraces of Christ who lives within them through his indwelling Spirit. This is why marriage is always ideally marriage unto death. Their fidelity to each other in both joy and sorrow is itself a sacramental symbol of God's love which is expressed in God's words to his people, "I have loved you with an everlasting love" (Jer 31:3).

The following quote from the Second Vatican Council's *Constitution on the Church in the Modern World* (No. 47) reflects the Church's continued awareness of the dignity and sanctity of married love, considered as a living sacrament of Christ's love for his church:

. . . a man and woman, who by their compact of conjugal love "are no longer two but one flesh" (Mt 19:6), render mutual help and service to each other through an intimate union of their persons and their actions. Through this union they experience the meaning of the oneness and attain to it with growing perfection day by day . . . . Christ the Lord abundantly blesses this many-faceted love, welling up as it does from the foundation of divine love and structured as it is on the model of his union with his Church. For as God of old made himself present to his people through a covenant of love and fidelity, so now the savior of men and the Spouse of the Church comes into the lives of married Christians through the sacrament of matrimony.

Activity and Discussion:

1.  It is no secret that divorce rates have been on the increase for quite some time. Many today, seeing this trend, feel a permanent, loving marriage relationship is practically impossible. Listed below are four areas that often prove to be areas of disagreement and tension in marriage. Gather into small groups and discuss each of these areas in terms of the following two points: 1. What attitudes, feelings, etc., are most likely to make this aspect of married life a source of disharmony? 2. What Christlike attitudes would make this area of married life less a matter of disunity and more an occasion of deeper sharing?

| AREA | ATTITUDES CAUSING DISUNITY | CHRISTIAN ATTITUDE |
|---|---|---|
| Money | | |
| In-laws | | |
| Boredom | | |
| Sensitivity to each other's needs | | |

2. Although you are always a member of your family, your family as a unit can drift apart. Special occasions are needed when the members of the family can gather together in ways that allow all involved to experience and deepen their love and commitment to one another.

As a class, make a list of as many such occasions, events, or experiences as you can think of. Then discuss: Why are such moments essential to the life of any family? What obstacles to such moments are present within us and within our society? How are such occasions kinds of *symbols* of family love?

## HOLY ORDERS

*Ordination.* The Book of Acts records how the twelve apostles carried out Christ's command to spread the Good News of Salvation. Also recorded is the presence of deacons, presbyters, and elders who assisted the apostles. Later these assistants assumed full responsibility for the service of leadership as the Church began to grow to the point where the apostles could not possibly do all the work themselves. Those who performed the ministry of leadership in its various forms were commissioned into service by the laying on of hands (Acts 6:6, 15:2; 1 Tim 3:8-12; Jas 21:18). It was recognized that all in the community were called to holiness, all shared in the priesthood of Christ by virtue of their baptism. But some were given charisms by the Holy Spirit to serve the community in special ways. That is, some were given gifts by the Holy Spirit to serve the believing community, to perform effectively important functions such as teaching, preaching, serving the sick and so forth.

Sometimes it is not clear exactly what these charisms entailed in terms of precise duties in the community. What is clear, however, is that by the third century Saint Cyprian expressed the Church's conviction that the twelve apostles were the first bishops and that the bishops of his day continued, each in his own community, to serve in the leadership role of the first apostles. *We also know that the primary task of the bishop was that of celebrating the Eucharist and of officiating at the other sacramental rites of the Church,* as well as serving the community in its other daily needs. We also know that others were selected to be ordained by the bishop to share in his priestly office. These assistants to the bishop in the celebration of the sacraments were the priests in the community.

Ordination to the priesthood involves first a basic decision to follow Christ in a manner that profoundly affects one's basic style of living. This decision begins first by a call (vocation) by the Holy Spirit which can be freely accepted or rejected. Once called, the person must, as it were, verify this calling by possessing the basic qualities that will be needed to serve the church as a priest. Finally, ordination itself places the seal of the Holy Spirit on those ordained, enabling them to carry out the rewarding, but sometimes demanding daily tasks of priestly ministry in the Church.

---

**EXERCISES:**

1. Make a list of what the class feels are the most difficult aspects about being a priest in the Church today. Then make out a list of the rewarding aspects of priesthood.

2. Today there is much talk about ordaining women and married men to the priesthood. A group in the class might want to research both of these areas and report on pros and cons of each.

---

## RECONCILIATION

The sacrament of reconciliation is a sacrament of healing. It finds its origin in the gospels in Jesus' words to his disciples,

> Receive the Holy Spirit.
> If you forgive men's sins, they are forgiven them;
> if you hold them bound, they are held bound.
>                                        (Jn 20:22-23)

In other words, the disciples received a direct mandate from Christ to continue to express his openness, compassion and forgiveness of sinners. The disciples were to be sacraments of healing forgiveness within the community (Mk 2:5-17, Lk 15; Mt 26:28).

The practice of receiving the sacrament of reconciliation has changed greatly in its long history in the Church. Originally, Baptism was considered the sacramental sign of forgiveness. In the early Church, Christian converts considered it unthinkable to betray Christ by sinning seriously. Soon, however, there appeared a separate rite of forgiveness of sins. This liturgical rite of forgiveness was not used except for the sins of adultery, murder and idolatry. The sacrament, which could be received only once in a person's lifetime, included the confession of the sin committed, a time of public prayer and penance, the laying on of hands (usually by the bishop), the pronouncing of the words of forgiveness and the joyful acceptance of the penitent back into the believing community. By the ninth century a major change occurred as the Irish monks began the practice of repeated, devotional, private confessions. In time this practice became the universally accepted form of receiving this sacrament in the Catholic Church.

In recent times, many Catholics have found it extremely difficult to find the reception of this sacrament a meaningful and helpful expression of their faith. As a consequence there has been a drastic decline in the number of Catholics receiving this sacrament.

In response to this need, the Church following the Second Vatican Council renewed the rite of penance. It made the sacrament more personal and meaningful by allowing for shared prayer, scripture reading and above all a time for honest dialogue between priest and penitent about whatever is hindering the penitent in his or her relationship to Christ. The option of anonymous confession through a screen remains but there is also provided the option of face-to-face confession. An emphasis is also given to communal penance services.

Because Christ has identified himself with the believing community of the Church, every sin we commit not only constitutes a weakening or breaking down of our life-giving relationship with Christ but also with the community in which we live. In this sacrament we, as social beings, return to the believing community, represented in the person of the priest. We do this to confess sincerely our sins and hear, in the words of the priest, Christ's own words of healing forgiveness.

---

For Discussion:

1. As a class, discuss the difficulties that arise in the reception of this sacrament due to the human frailty both of the priests and ourselves. What are some ways these difficulties can be faced and overcome? Compare them to the difficulties encountered in any expression of sincere in-depth dialogue.

2. Together share experiences those in the group may have had with communal penance services. What is the significance of celebrating the sacrament of reconciliation as a community?

---

## ANOINTING OF THE SICK

This sacrament, like the sacrament of reconciliation, is a sacrament of healing. It finds its New Testament basis in Jesus' concern for the sick. We also read in the New Testament that the disciples of Jesus anointed the sick with oil as a sign of the healing power of Christ (Mk 6:31; Jas 5:14-15). There are also clear references in the liturgical rites of the early Church that indicated that the anointing of the sick was a sacramental action of Christ in the community. In the Middle Ages, the sacrament became, for all practical purposes, the anointing of those on their deathbeds. It was not administered unless the person was actually dying.

Today the Church has returned to a more biblical understanding of this sacrament which is that of bringing Christ's ongoing healing power to the sick. It is the sacrament of the sick rather than of the dying. As such, it is aimed at restoring the sick person to health physically, mentally and/or spiritually, including the forgiveness of sins, because of the power of Christ present in the sacrament. Christ strengthens the faithful who in this sacrament turn to him in their hour of illness and need. They thus become a sacramental sign to the whole community of Christ's enduring presence in the community.

For Discussion:

Today, many speak of the old and infirm as being use-
less. What do you think these members of the Christian
community have to offer the rest of us? What do they
remind us about ourselves? What can we and should we
offer them in return? How is the anointing of the sick a
*sacramental* expression of these Christian concerns?

## THE SACRAMENTS OF LIFE

Among the routine, often humdrum, events of daily life there
stand those vitally important moments and events which form the
focal points of our lives. In these moments we are always, in some
way, intimately involved with others, especially our family and/or
friends. As we saw in this chapter, Jesus in the seven sacraments
touches and transforms these key moments of human life into living
encounters with himself.

**EXERCISE:**

Do the following exercise in small groups and then share your answers as a class. Your task is to jot down a word or phrase you think best describes our relationship to both friends/family and Jesus in each of the key moments of life and their corresponding sacramental celebration. (This exercise is adapted from Richard Reichart, *Teaching the Sacraments to Youth.* New York: Paulist, 1975, p. 96)

| Life Event | Friends', Family's relationship or involvement | Sacrament | How Jesus transforms this moment into an expression of our relationship with him |
|---|---|---|---|
| BIRTH | | BAPTISM | |
| NOURISHMENT | | EUCHARIST | |
| STRENGTHEN-ING AND GROWTH | | CONFIRMA-TION | |
| MARRIAGE | | MATRIMONY | |
| ROLE IN THE COMMUNITY | | ORDERS | |
| FAILURES | | RECONCILIA-TION | |
| SICKNESS/ DEATH | | HEALING | |

## WHAT DOES THIS MEAN?

An underlying question in this whole discussion on the sacraments might very likely be one of an honest inability to find the presence of Christ in the sacraments. This question might be phrased as, "Why is it that if Christ is present in the sacraments, I find the Mass boring, the sacrament of reconciliation unnecessary and the sacraments in general alien to my personal religious experience?" The following exercise is offered as a means of answering this question.

On the board make seven columns, letting each column represent one of the sacraments. All should turn to p. 118 of this chapter. There you will find listed four essential elements of our ability to appreciate and enter into any kind of human sign. After a brief discussion to review the four requirements for appreciating signs, break up into seven groups (if there are not enough students to do this, the sacraments can be divided up among a smaller number of groups). Each group should apply the four points to the sacraments assigned to it. The exercise should end by each group sharing its ideas with the class, and allowing the other class members to add their own comments.

A second question about the sacraments is a parallel to the first. Sometimes it is not our shortcomings that prevent us from entering into the sacrament but rather the shortcoming of the parish in which we live. In response to this problem, we must first make a comparison to any human relationship and point out that in our weakness we never measure up to the ideal. But if our love is sincere, we do not allow these failings to destroy the relationship itself. A wife does not leave her husband because he snores, nor do parents desert their teenage children because they happen to eat too much. So, too, possible failings in the leaders of the parish is no reason to simply ignore and walk away from the celebration of the sacraments. Christ lives in us and speaks through us in spite of our shared weakness. Then, too, it is good to pause and reflect on what you can do actively to better the quality of sacramental celebrations in your school, religious education program or parish. Instead of complaining about the lack of such things as youth Masses, communal penance services and the like, you, with your friends, can find out what you can do to improve the situation.

## OTHER QUESTIONS

The emphasis the Catholic Church gives to the sacraments raises the question of the place of the sacraments in the Protestant traditions of Christianity. The number and diversity of Protestant denominations prevent us from giving any one single answer to this question. In general, however, we can say that most Protestant denominations have a deep appreciation for the presence of Christ living in the believing community and especially in the living Word of scripture. And thus, in this general sense, they share with us our sense of the sacramental presence of Jesus available to us.

More practically, we find that Martin Luther himself held firmly the real presence of Christ in the Eucharist and that he said sacraments were "the bridge, the path, the way, the ladder by which the Spirit might come to you." The sacraments of Baptism and Eucharist are celebrated in practically all Protestant churches. And although some denominations deny that the Eucharist is actually the presence of Christ, theologians in other denominations, such as the Lutherans and the United Methodists have stated their belief in the real presence of Christ in their celebrations of the Lord's Supper. Luther's theme of the "bible alone" and the subsequent rejection of much that developed in the tradition of the Church often led to the dropping of the other five sacraments considered as actual sacraments in the same sense of Baptism and Eucharist. Surely, many obstacles remain to be overcome before the Protestants and Catholics can maintain their own heritages and yet express a unity in creed, moral teaching and worship (celebration of the sacraments). In respecting these real differences the Catholic Church does not yet allow the open communion between Catholics and Protestants. But great strides are being made on both sides. The Fathers of the Second Vatican Council in the *Constitution on the Church* expressed the desire for the union of all Christians saying,

> They (the Protestants) are consecrated by Baptism in which they are united to Christ. They also receive other sacraments in their own churches or ecclesiastical communities . . . In all of Christ's disciples the Spirit arouses the desire and effort to be peacefully united in the manner determined by Christ, as one flock under one shepherd.
>
> (No. 15)

## SUMMARY

1. Signs point to or indicate some other reality. Symbols, in some way, contain and bring about what they signify.

2. God is immanent in his creation and thus the universe and all that is in it is in some way a symbol of God's presence.

3. To be sensitive to symbols we must have the proper attitudes.

4. A sacrament is a very special symbol in which we encounter God. Jesus is the perfect sacrament of God. And the Church is the sacrament of the risen Jesus.

5. The seven sacraments are seven moments or seven events in which we encounter the risen Jesus living in the believing community.

   a. In Baptism we receive the Holy Spirit and are made members of the community of the Church.

   b. Confirmation emphasizes the power of the Holy Spirit to change us into strong, fully committed disciples of Christ.

   c. The Eucharist, with Baptism and Confirmation, forms the third sacrament of initiation. But the Eucharist is received throughout life as a constant reminder that Jesus is our nourishment on the way to the Father.

   d. In matrimony Christ is made the living center of the family and of the love a husband and wife have for each other.

   e. Holy Orders celebrates Christ's presence in the unique service and ministry that priests have within the community.

f. In Reconciliation Christ heals us of the alienation of sin.

g. The sacrament of the sick celebrates Christ's continual healing presence even in the face of sickness, old age and death.

## EVALUATION

In light of all you have learned in this chapter, go back to the opening exercise on p. 114 and expand and reword your original answers. As a class share what you feel are the most striking aspects about the sacraments that you have learned.

**ADDITIONAL EXERCISES:**

1. Invite a priest to come into the class to explain the actual rites of the sacraments. Special attention can be given to the historical significance of the changes introduced since the Second Vatican Council. Emphasis can be given to one sacrament by having the rite either acted out or actually performed with the class. For example, the class can have a communal penance or a classroom liturgy.

2. Research the "signs" of other religions. Note how these signs differ and are similiar to the sacraments and sacramentals of the Catholic faith.

3. Examine different kinds of music and different kinds of art from our own and other times and cultures. How are art and music important forms of signs? How is this reflected in Church art and music?

# 6

# Christian Morality:
# Living a Christian Life

*My point is that you should live in accord with the spirit and you will not yield to the cravings of the flesh. The flesh lusts against the spirit and the spirit against the flesh; the two are directly opposed. This is why you do not do what your will intends. If you are guided by the spirit, you are not under the law. It is obvious what proceeds from the flesh: lewd conduct, impurity, licentiousness, idolatry, sorcery, hostilities, bickering, jealousy, outbursts of rage, selfish rivalries, dissensions, factions, envy, drunkenness, orgies, and the like. I warn you, as I have warned you before: those who do such things will not inherit the kingdom of God.*

*In contrast, the fruit of the spirit is love, joy, peace, patient endurance, kindness, generosity, faith, mildness, and chastity.*

(Gal 5:16-23)

Christian morality can be summarized by the word *responsibility.* As a result, Christian morality has two components, namely, *response* and the *ability* to respond. To what does the Christian respond? A Christian responds to God's incredible, freely given love and his gift of salvation offered to us through our Lord Jesus Christ. This salvation cannot in any way be earned; it is entirely a gift on the part of the Father. As St. Paul says: "But God is rich in mercy; because of his great love for us he brought us to life with Christ when we were dead in sin. By this favor you were saved" (Eph 2:4-5). We cannot earn this love because it is already ours; it is entirely a gift.

141

God, however, respects our freedom.  He does not thrust his loving gift of salvation on us as though we were mere puppets to be toyed with.  He extends his love freely.  Christian morality comes to the forefront when people say YES to God, that is, when they respond to his love.  What, in essence, is the nature of this response to love?  What is the essence of Christian morality?  It is, simply, *love*.  Listen to the words of Jesus himself:

> You shall love the Lord your God
>     with your whole heart,
> with your whole soul,
>     and with your whole mind.
> This is the greatest and first commandment.
>     The second is like it:
>     You shall love your neighbor as yourself.
>                                     (Mt 22:37-39)

The other side of the coin in Christian morality is the *ability* to respond to God, the ability to love, the ability to say yes to God.  This ability is itself a gift, also freely bestowed on us.  Christian morality does not rest primarily on our own talents, strengths, insights or deeds.  Rather, true Christian morality is rooted in the Holy Spirit who has been given to us at baptism.  The Father has given us not only the summons to love, but also the power of God's own love—the Holy Spirit—with which to respond. ". . . The love of God has been poured out in our hearts through the Holy Spirit who has been given to us" (Rm 5:5).

By saying that Christian morality is responsibility regarding God's invitation to life and to love, we are really saying that Christian morality is bound up with the *covenant* relationship between God and his children.  The purpose of this chapter will be to discuss the covenantal nature of Christian morality.  After defining and clarifying the meaning of covenant, we will discuss the following three questions:

1. How does the Christian respond to God's call of love? (The Ten Commandments and the Beatitudes.)

2. What is personal conscience? (The ability to choose right from wrong; the ability to discover God's will for me.)

3. What is sin? (A failure of covenant love.)

But before we launch into these topics, please reflect on and discuss the following exercises which will help you to think about Christian morality.

---

**EXERCISES:**

1. One of the first and most important principles of Christian morality is summed up in the statement: *To be moral is to be human.* That principle, of course, hinges on one's definition of what it means to be human. Both reason and revelation help us define and describe what a human is. A clear, refreshingly optimistic view of the human person can be found in Vatican II's *Gaudium et Spes,* the "Pastoral Constitution on the Church in the Modern World." You may wish to read that document now, especially sections 12-17. Here is a very brief summary of those paragraphs:

Human persons have a *basic dignity* which flows from their being created in God's image (with a soul); this implies that we can *think* and *love* and are in *relationship to others in community* (12). We are created with bodies (*body-persons*) which are *fundamentally good* (14), though we are *inclined to sin* (13). Our *conscience,* "the most secret core and sanctuary of man" (16), aids us in a life directed to God and other people. And, finally, it is in our *freedom of choice* (17) where we assert our basic dignity because it is that which directs us to the good.

In light of this Christian definition of human beings, mark those activities which you think are immoral because they deny or minimize what it means to be human. Discuss these with your classmates.

　　　　——— 1. smoking pot
　　　　——— 2. smoking pot without
　　　　　　　parental permission
　　　　——— 3. driving a car
　　　　——— 4. cheating at sports
　　　　——— 5. cheating on tests
　　　　——— 6. dating
　　　　——— 7. cussing
　　　　——— 8. using obscene
　　　　　　　gestures

——— 9. taking shortcuts on the job

———10. drinking alcohol underage

———11. not praying

———12. laughing at a teacher who was mocked out

———13. spending money on records

———14. not exercising

———15. going to a bar/dance hall which excludes members of certain minorities

———16. making jokes about homosexuals

———17. taking the "easiest math teacher"

———18. choosing to go to a costly college away from home

2. The following is a moral dilemma. Individually decide what Tom Johnson should do. Then list reasons for your choice. In small groups, see if you can come up with a consensus as to what he should do. Finally, discuss the case with the whole class, outlining the validity of reasons given.

*CASE:* Tom Johnson is a senior who is in charge of all the prom arrangements. He is held in the highest esteem by his classmates and by the faculty as well. One day, a week or so before the prom, his girl-friend, Sue, informs him in strictest confidence that several of their classmates plan to come to the after-prom and dispense "uppers" to anyone who wants them. Sue and others have tried to talk the people involved out of their proposed activity, but to no avail. Because of some serious trouble at last year's prom which resulted in the death of a student, the administration of the school has told Tom and other seniors that if any drugs are used either at the prom or the after-prom, the school will cease sponsoring the prom or any prom-related event for a two-year period. What is Tom to do? What reasons do you give for your choice?

(Have your parents solve this same dilemma. Discuss with them the reasons for their choices.)

3. In the Middle Ages, medieval knights used to abide by a code of chivalry which animated everything they did. In the highly successful Broadway musical *Man of La Mancha,* Don Quixote tried to live by the following code of conduct:

Call nothing thy own except thy soul.
Love not what thou art, but only what thou
   may become.
Do not pursue pleasure, for thou may have
   the misfortune to overtake it.
Look always forward; in last year's nest
   there are no birds this year.
Be just to all men.  Be courteous to all
   women.
Live in the Vision of that one for whom
   great deeds are done . . .
            —Dale Wasserman, Joe Darion and
              Mitch Leigh. *Man of La Mancha*
              (New York: Random House, 1966),
              p. 47.

a. Discuss Quixote's code.  Is it realistic?  Does it sound Christian?

b. Write a short paragraph or poem which reflects your code of morality, that is, how you try to live and to relate to other people and to God.

Share these with your classmates.

---

## KEY TEACHINGS

## HOW DOES THE CHRISTIAN RESPOND TO GOD'S LOVE?

### Christian Morality is Covenantal

The key insight of Christian morality which helps to distinguish it from other moralities and ethical systems is that it is based on a covenant relationship.  A covenant is the strongest possible mutual pledge between two parties (often of unequal rank) wherein certain commitments are made.  The Old Testament reveals Yahweh as a God of covenant who entered into a number of loving relationships with mankind in general and the Jews in particular. For example, the covenant with Noah (Gn 9:8-17) was a promise on Yahweh's part to continue life on earth.  The covenant with Abraham (Gn 15:17) resulted in the promise of numerous posterity and a land—the land of Canaan.  A very special covenant was the Sinai covenant (Ex 6:8; Lv 26:12; Dt 26:17f).  In the Sinai covenant, Israel was blessed as Yahweh's special people.  She became for all people everywhere the *sign* of God's promise, a God who delivered an oppressed people and kept them alive against insurmountable odds. As a result, Israel was described as a kingdom of priests whose relationship with Yahweh is depicted in terms of a father and son (Ex 4:22f) or in the intimate bond of husband and wife.

The covenant with David intensified and formalized the Sinai covenant. "I will be his father and he my son" (2 Sam 7:14; Ps 89:27; 2:7). The love relationship between Yahweh and his people had moved beyond mere preservation of a species or the giving of a land or the calling of a special people. The relationship had become a blood relationship—a relationship that was to be written on mankind's heart (Jer 21:27).

Because a covenant always implied commitments, for his part Yahweh promised to be faithful to his word. In return, Yahweh wanted his people to live a life of faithfulness to the covenant. He desired that men and women live as though they were specially blessed and called to witness to him, the one true God. For the Jews, this meant that living the Law was a way to *respond* to God, a way to say "yes" to the special gifts God bestowed on them as a people. The Law, and more specifically the Ten Commandments, were not seen as a list of burdensome obligations to be tolerated, but rather a way to live out the special identity bestowed on them. If you are a special people, then your behavior will be special. When you act in a loving, responsive way, you will be a prayerful sign to all peoples that there is a loving, caring God who desires all of humanity to be one with him.

The New Testament covenant is the new mutual pledge in Christ's blood (Mk 14:24). Jesus' death and resurrection seals our relationship with the Father. It is the most important covenant of all for the Spirit given to us at baptism enables us to call God "Father." As St. Paul writes:

> The proof that you are sons is the fact that God
> has sent forth into our hearts the spirit of his Son

which cries "Abba" ("Father!").  You are no longer
a slave but a son!  And the fact that you are a son
makes you an heir, by God's design.

(Gal 4:6-7)

The Christian responds to his vocation as a child of God in
two ways: first, by living the Ten Commandments, for as Jesus
said: "Whoever fulfills and teaches these commands shall be great
in the kingdom of God" (Mt 5:19).  Second, the Christian is true
to his or her identity by trying to live the Sermon on the Mount as
summarized in the Eight Beatitudes.  For the Christian, these are
not burdensome lists to be obeyed but rather joyous opportunities
to say "yes" to the love and call of a loving Father.

## The Ten Commandments

The Ten Commandments are found in Ex 20:2-17 and Dt
5:6-21.  The summary listed here is a widely used version.  Below
we will discuss briefly each commandment as a way to respond to
our vocation as adopted sons and daughters of the Father.

1. I, the Lord, am your God.  You shall not have other gods
   besides me.

2. You shall not take the name of the Lord, your God, in
   vain.

3. Remember to keep holy the sabbath day.

4. Honor your father and your mother.

5. You shall not kill.

6. You shall not commit adultery.

7. You shall not steal.

8. You shall not bear false witness against your neighbor.

9. You shall not covet your neighbor's wife.

10. You shall not covet anything that belongs to your
    neighbor.

*First Three Commandments:*

"Love God above all things."

1. The first commandment helps us put things in perspective. It means, simply, that God must be the goal of human life. Our ultimate life goal is to be united with him forever. All too often humans substitute something else for God and make it the be-all and end-all of their existence. Sex, money, power, prestige—these are all good in their place—but when we end up worshipping them, we have failed to recognize the one who created them; thus, we are unfaithful. The Christian puts his or her faith in God and God alone, not in substitute gods like astrological charts, good luck charms, witchcraft and the like. God alone is the source of life and meaning and the Christian is true to this God.

2. The second commandment deals with respect in the use of God's name and our manner of worship. The Christian realizes that one's speech reflects who one is. Some things are sacred, including God's name, and our language should manifest this careful respect. Our attitude in prayer, too, should be one of humility in approaching God. We pray in confident humility that God's will be done; the Christian does not heap up a lot of words that demand that God do his or her will.

3. Faithfulness to God dictates that we adore him, and adore him with others. Since humans are social beings, it stands to reason that they should join together when they approach their creator. Salvation is not something we work at in isolation from others. In the Christian community, we realize the extreme importance of approaching God the Father with our Savior Jesus joined together in the Holy Spirit. Thus, the Mass is very special for the Christian community. Christians realize that one hour out of a 168-hour week is a minimum amount of time to set aside if we are to grow closer to God. We do this on Sunday, the day of the Lord's resurrection.

*Last Seven Commandments:*

"Love your neighbor as yourself."

4. The covenant between Christians and God is reflected in the family. Just as God loves people, so should parents love and care for their children, educating them and giving them sufficient freedom to grow into independence. So, too, should children offer respect, obedience, courtesy and gratitude to their parents. Likewise, brothers and sisters owe each other patience, friendship and respect so that the family might be a harmonious community of love. This commandment also has social ramifications in that all proper authority is deserving of our obedience and respect since all authority ultimately comes from God.

5. The greatest gift God gave us is the gift of life. The fifth commandment stresses our need to safeguard the life God has granted to us. In regard to our own lives, we must take care of our bodies, for example, by eating proper food, by getting enough rest and relaxation, by avoiding harmful substances and dangerous practices. Similarly, the Christian is very concerned to protect the lives of others, especially innocent human life. Jesus showed that God's love extends in a special way to the weak and helpless. Thus, Christians recognize the seriousness of pro-life issues such as war, abortion and euthanasia.

6. Covenant love, so often likened to the love between a husband and wife in the Old Testament, extends also to Christian marriage. Unfaithfulness is unbecoming covenant love; in a marriage, adultery is the great act of unfaithfulness. Christians are also called by this commandment to respect the procreative powers with which God blessed them. Sexual love is a share in God's own creative act. Thus, acts which exploit others or which are indulged in selfishly are out of place for God's children. The virtue the sixth commandment extols is *chastity,* that is, respectful self-control that preserves one's capacity to see and to fulfill one's sexuality in a perspective of love.

7. Theft of any kind destroys trust. As God's children, we are entitled to the gifts of creation which we honestly attain. To steal is to break down smooth human relationships needed for harmonious and peaceful living. Cheating and shoplifting are two forms of theft most prevalent in the world today. Cheating in the classroom, for example, destroys the trusting environment needed for educational growth. Shoplifting has widespread social effects, for example, in higher prices for everyone. In a real way, failing to use our God-given talents and abilities is a form of theft. By not developing our gifts we keep others from sharing something good given to us to enrich not only ourselves but others as well.

8. The touchstone of a person's character is one's honesty. For the Christian to be honest is to witness to the truth. Revenge, gossip, scandal and lies all help destroy the covenant love which helps bind together the human community. Love of neighbor often means witnessing to the truth because the truth sets us free.

9. and 10. Covetousness refers to obsessive lusting. Lust is often motivated by jealousy, materialism or self-indulgence. Inordinate and uncontrolled internal desires in the area of sex or material possessions can breed hate and rivalry. They are destructive and color a person's entire outlook on life. These two commandments stress the importance of pure intention and decent motives when relating to others. The external act which violates love flows from an internal desire left unchecked.

**EXERCISE:**

Below are listed violations of the covenant love preserved in the Ten Commandments. Utilizing a resource book like the *Catholic Encyclopedia,* Fr. John Hardon's *The Catholic Catechism* (Garden City, New York: Doubleday & Company, Inc., 1975), *An American Catholic Catechism* (New York: The Seabury Press, 1975), *The Teaching of Christ* (Huntington, Indiana: Our Sunday Visitor Press, 1976) or some similar resource book, find out the following three things:

a. A definition of the term;
b. An example;
c. A comment or two on how that act destroys covenant love.

Divide the topics up and give a *report* to the class.

1. Divination (spiritualism)
   Magic
   Sorcery
   Satanism
   Sacrilege
   Simony

2. Oath-taking
   Breaking vows
   Blasphemy
   Cursing

3. Servile work on
   Sunday

4. Disobedience
   Disrespect

5. Euthanasia
   Abortion
   War
   Capital punishment

(5. con't)
   Sterilization
   Suicide
   Murder
   Genetic engineer-
      ing
   Eugenics

6. Adultery
   Fornication
   Divorce
   Artificial means of
      contraception

7. Embezzlement
   Looting
   Larceny
   Price fixing

8. Insult
   Calumny
   Detraction
   Rash judgment

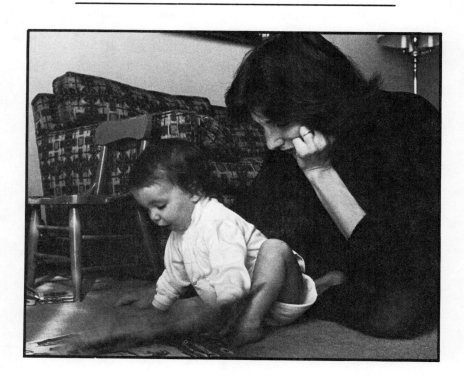

## THE BEATITUDES

Christians have always held the Beatitudes of Jesus in the highest esteem for they summarize well the morality all Christians should try to live in their response both to God and to neighbor. The Beatitudes introduce the finest summary of New Testament teaching concerning Christian behavior, namely, the Sermon on the Mount (Mt 5:7). Jesus, unlike some ethical teachers of his day, did not try to give a detailed list of rules and regulations his disciples were to follow. Rather, he gave general guidelines which get at the basic attitudes his followers should have in relationship to other people and to their God. The Beatitudes are the most graphic example of these underlying attitudes of mind and heart which should guide all response to God's invitation to love. The Beatitudes and a brief explanation of each are listed below.

1. How blest are the poor in spirit: the reign of God is theirs.

2. Blest too are the sorrowing; they shall be consoled.

3. Blest are the lowly; they shall inherit the land.

4. Blest are they who hunger and thirst for holiness; they shall have their fill.

5. Blest are they who show mercy; mercy shall be theirs.

6. Blest are the single-hearted for they shall see God.

7. Blest are the peacemakers; they shall be called sons of God.

8. Blest are those persecuted for holiness' sake; the reign of God is theirs.

(Mt 5:3-10)

## THE BEATITUDES EXPLAINED

1. One of the signs that the kingdom of God had broken into human history was that it was announced to the poor. Jesus himself had special affection for the downtrodden and the unfortunate. The lesson of this beatitude is plain. Those who are deprived of material goods, power, prestige and the like tend to relate to God more easily, are inclined to trust him completely. Thus, in praising the poor in spirit, Jesus teaches his followers to be absolutely confident and trusting of God alone. The things we acquire, the prestigious name we have, the power we have over people—all of these in the last analysis are worthless. Our salvation and future are found by trusting and obeying the Father.

2. The second beatitude gives hope that in the midst of our trials and difficulties at school, at work, in our relationships with others, we will be eventually consoled. Patient suffering and endurance of our trials does have its reward, despite what modern advertisements and the media wish to teach us.

3. "Meek" in the Bible use of the term does not mean a "pious milksop." Rather, the meek or lowly person is one who is humble, who does not resort to jealousy and actions menacing to others when he or she is hurt and despised. In short, the meek or lowly person is nonviolent. Elsewhere in the Sermon on the Mount (Mt 5:38-48), Jesus challenges his followers to solve their problems nonviolently by turning the other cheek. This is one of the great calls Jesus makes to Christians: to solve one's problems without hatred, rancor, ill will or violence.

4. One of the tasks of all disciples of Jesus is to get involved in the affairs of the world. "Hunger and thirsting for holiness" means "hungering and thirsting for righteousness," for justice. The Christian has an active call to work for God's kingdom, not merely in a passive way by enduring personal wrongs, but in an active way seeing to it that all of God's children are treated with respect, dignity and equality.

5. In the great Christian prayer the "Our Father," we ask God "to forgive us our sins as we forgive the sins of those who have wronged us." The Father's unbelievable love has been given to us without our ever deserving it. The love manifests itself in his forgiving us our sins and accepting us into his family as adopted sons and daughters. As a result, he expects his children to extend mercy, love and forgiveness to those who have hurt us, even our enemies. This is perhaps the most difficult mandate of Christian living. But in responding to it we show to all people that ours is a loving, merciful God who cares for all.

6. The single-hearted are those who let nothing get in the way of their commitment to God. "To love with one's whole heart, one's whole mind, one's whole soul," means that nothing else—no matter how good—should distract us from God. Sex, money, our jobs, even other people, all of which are good, should play a secondary role in our lives. Only doing God's will in all things should take precedence.

7. This beatitude also puts emphasis on the active role a Christian should take in the world. Jesus came to bring peace to the world. Christians are obligated to imitate him, that is, to try and unite those who are in strife, disharmony and opposition. Such people will be called children of God since, for men and women, the divine call is to divine brotherhood and sisterhood with Jesus Christ. Our obligation in charity is to love not only those whom we like or who like us or who are related to us, but to love those who are difficult to love: the poor, the despised, our enemies and those who have wronged us. Proof of love is to make peace among our brothers and sisters; love and peace are signs of the divine sonship and daughterhood which is ours.

8. A real sign of union with our Lord is to suffer and be persecuted for him. Just as our Lord's deeds and words brought him misunderstanding and abuse, so for those who walk in the way of the Lord. We must be willing to stand for our convictions, even if this means rejection, verbal abuse, martyrdom. The promised reward is God's kingdom itself.

**EXERCISE:**

Read and study the Sermon on the Mount, Mt 5-7. The Sermon on the Mount goes into more detail in exemplifying the kinds of attitudes the Christian should have in response to God and neighbor. In fact, one way of looking at the beatitudes is to reflect on the term "be-attitudes." As Christians, our attitude of being is that of living out our call as children of the heavenly Father whom we call Abba, daddy. As a result, in all of our moral actions, we should *be* children of God and brothers and sisters of Jesus and one another. Our attitude should be one of striving to be perfect as the heavenly Father is perfect, that is, trying today a bit harder than yesterday to live a responsible life.

In light of your study of the Sermon on the Mount, judge which one in the pair of choices reflects more a "beatitude mentality." Offer reasons for your choice. Then, as a class, see if you can arrive at a consensus for each pair.

1. — a. helping in a first-aid situation without proper training
   b. refusing to help in a first-aid situation until getting properly trained

2. — a. giving $10 for flood victims without anyone knowing about it
   — b. giving $50 for flood victims telling only a best friend

3. — a. becoming a social worker for low pay
   — b. becoming a high-paid businessperson and giving 10% of one's salary to the poor

4. — a. having 4 children of one's own
   — b. adopting 2 children

5. — a. refusing to eat junk food
   — b. fasting once a week

# WHAT IS PERSONAL CONSCIENCE?

Thankfully, all people have been given a guide in discovering the right or the wrong. This guide is conscience—myself judging whether an action or an attitude is right or wrong, an ability to discover God's will for me. Conscience has been defined by the Church fathers as the most secret core and sanctuary of my person. It is there that we are alone with God whose voice echoes in our hearts.

Another way to look at conscience is that within us there is an inner dialogue with God who calls us to be the persons we are intended to be, his children.

The key principle in a discussion of conscience can be summed up in the brief phrase: conscience must be *formed* and *followed*. Conscience must be *followed* because it is the final arbiter in making moral decisions. The "Pastoral Constitution on the Church in the Modern World" puts it this way:

> In the depths of his conscience, man detects a law which he does not impose upon himself, but which holds him to obedience. Always summoning him to love good and do it and to avoid evil, the voice of conscience can when necessary speak to his heart more specifically: do this, shun that. For man has in his heart a law written by God. *To obey it is the very dignity of man: according to it he will be judged.* (16)

By the same token, a conscience should be *formed*. "In this regard I too always strive to keep my conscience clear before God and man" (Acts 24:16). Note Vatican II says that the law within is not imposed upon a person by himself or herself. We are all prone to make mistakes when left to ourselves. Many factors can help cloud up a conscience and make it difficult to choose right from wrong; factors like *ignorance,* that is, simply not knowing or being told the right thing to do or the wrong thing to avoid. Strong *emotions* also cloud up a conscience. For example, at times we may be tempted to do things because "it feels good"—but feeling good does not necessarily mean that something is right. *Conformity* to what others are doing also muddies up conscience decisions. Just because "the crowd is doing it" does not make it right.

How do we form our consciences? Below is a checklist which might help in studying the factors that need to be considered in a properly formed conscience. Before examining the list, let us pose a case which is a "conscience case." Apply the steps of good conscience formation to this case. Decide individually what should be done and then discuss the case with your classmates.

CASE: Grandfather Jones lives with his daughter, her husband and five children. He is 70 years old and in failing health. He is starting to think he is a burden on the family. He is seriously contemplating taking an overdose of sleeping pills, in this case a form of euthanasia (or suicide) in order to ease family tensions. Would this be the right thing for him to do?

— 1. *Find the facts. What* is the issue? *Who* is involved? *Where? When? How?*

— 2. *Examine the motives. Why* does one propose to do this? Intentions are very important in morality.

— 3. *Think of the possible effects.* How will this action (nonaction) affect myself, others, society as a whole?

— 4. *Consider alternatives.* Might there be another way out of the dilemma? Use imagination to come up with other solutions.

— 5. *What does the law have to say?* Law is not opposed to conscience. As a matter of fact, it greatly helps to form it. Whereas conscience is the subjective norm of morality, law is the objective norm. Good law is always *reasonable, given by proper authority* in a way that *people know about it,* and is *ultimately for the common good.* The kinds of law which need to be considered are:

   a. *Natural Law:* God's law written into the nature of things, the way things are made. Prohibitions against murder or the recognition of the dignity of the individual are examples of natural law.

   b. *Civil Law:* Particular applications of natural law for a given society. E.g., in the United States, everyone drives on the right side of the road (civil law) in order to avoid killing others (natural law). In England, motorists drive on the left side of the road. There, the civil law differs.

    c. *Divine Law:* Law revealed by God. The Sermon on the Mount is a classic example of divine law, especially the law to love.

    d. *Church Law:* Particular applications of divine law for the Christian community.

— 6. *What is the reasonable thing to do?* Because we are people with minds, we must use them.

— 7. *What does my experience and that of other people say about the issue?* Because we are social beings with a history we must check out other responses to similar problems. We do have the obligation to seek out wise counsel.

— 8. *What would Jesus have done?* How does this measure up to his yardstick of love? In addition, what does the New Testament have to say? Jesus is the *absolute norm* of Christian morality. He is the one perfect human response to God, the Father. We have the strict obligation to seek out his will and his example before making a decision.

— 9. *What is the teaching of the Church?* We believe that the Holy Spirit resides in the Church and helps guide us in right behavior. The pope, bishops, councils, theologians, teachers, all have something to say about moral issues.

—10. *Pray for guidance.*

—11. *Admit that I am a sinner and might be wrong.* As St. Paul says, one of the effects of original sin is that the good I wish I would do, I don't do and the evil I wish to avoid, I do. As a result, ask for God's forgiveness.

—12. *After all of this, weigh the facts sincerely, judge the facts fairly,* and *act on the facts wisely,* that is, follow your conscience.

After all of this, what if someone goes against his or her conscience? It is always wrong to go against one's conscience. "When a man knows the right thing to do and does not do it, he sins" (Jas 4:17). Sin will be topic for discussion in the next section of the chapter.

---

**EXERCISE:**

In this section of the chapter, we discussed briefly the topic of conscience and mentioned that law helps form conscience. We noted the following qualities of good law: It is reasonable; given by proper authority; published in a way that people know about it; and directed to the common good. We also mentioned various kinds of law, including Church Law. Below are listed some of the Church Laws which we in the Catholic community observe. Discuss how each law is:

    a. reasonable for the Catholic;

    b. helpful for the common good.

1. To keep holy the day of the Lord's resurrection: to worship God by participating in Mass every Sunday and Holy Days of Obligation: to avoid those activities that would hinder renewal of soul and body, e.g., needless work and business activities, unnecessary shopping, etc.

2. To lead a sacramental life: to receive Holy Communion frequently and the Sacrament of Penance regularly—minimally, to receive the Sacrament of Penance at least once a year (annual confession is obligatory only if serious sin is involved).
—minimally, to receive Holy Communion at least once a year, between the First Sunday of Lent and Trinity Sunday.

3. To study Catholic teaching in preparation for the Sacrament of Confirmation, to be confirmed, and then to study and advance the cause of Christ.

4. To observe the marriage laws of the Church: to give religious training (by example and word) to one's children; to use parish schools and religious education programs.

5. To strengthen and support the Church: one's own parish community and parish priests; the worldwide Church and the Holy Father.

6. To do penance, including abstaining from meat and fasting from food on appointed days.

7. To join in the missionary spirit and apostolate of the Church.

(Taken from *Basic Teachings for Catholic Religious Education.* U.S. Catholic Conference, 1973, p. 28.)

---

Apply the 12 points of conscience formation to the following "Conscience situations":

- whether to cheat on a test knowing that many other students are cheating and ruining the curve

- whether to leave the scene of a minor accident in a parking lot when there are no witnesses

- whether to dismantle the pollution control devices on one's car to get better gas mileage

- whether to read pornographic literature

- whether to attend Sunday Mass even when you don't want to

---

## WHAT IS SIN?

The physical sickness that we see in hospitals mirrors the spiritual sickness called sin we also experience. Sin is a failure to love ourselves, others and God. Sin is an important concept for the Christian. Without a healthy concept of sin, people tend to see little need for Jesus. This is so because we call Jesus our Savior, one who saves us from sin. If we are unable to admit there is sin in the world or that we are capable of it, then it is quite understandable why some would not be attracted to the one who heals us from sin, rescues us from its effects, and overcomes it. Christians do not harp on sin out of a morbid attraction to evil and the absence of love. Bad news is not what our message is about. Rather, we talk of sin in order to stress the good news that our loving Father forgives us and in the person of Jesus has rescued us from its greatest effect, physical death.

There are two basic categories of sin: original sin and personal sin. Original sin was discussed in Chapter 1. Suffice it to say here that original sin refers to that condition of disharmony caused by being born into sin. This condition is inherited. "It is human nature so fallen, stripped of the grace that clothed it, injured in its own natural powers and subjected to the dominion of death" (Pope Paul VI, *Credo of the People of God*, #16). Universal human experience confirms the Catholic teaching that we are born into a sinful state. The evil we see around us, the anger we have within us toward others and self, the good intentions we so often break are all evidences of the sin which is part of humanity's condition.

*Personal sin* can be explained by way of a diagram. The oval represents a relationship. Bounded within the relationship is God and man united in covenant love (a). This is a graced relationship.

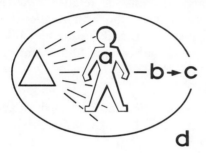

Grace is the gift of God's own life which makes us holy (sanctifying). We cannot earn it; it is freely given on God's part. This is the good news Jesus came to preach. His father loves us infinitely and wants us united to him. We need but turn to the Father, give up our sinful ways, and accept his love (*metanoia*). When we do this, we have a loving relationship with the Father. His offer is always there because his love is *always* there. We need but accept the offer.

Personal sin can be looked at in terms of weakening this love relationship or killing it (Is 1:2). Traditionally, *venial sin* refers to those acts and attitudes which do one of two things: (1) fail to help us grow in our loving relationship; or (2) weaken the relationship (*b* in the diagram). People have often somewhat glibly talked of "I only committed a venial sin." This is false thinking because any weakening of a love relationship is something to be concerned about. A friend who has hurt his relationship with another through some sarcastic remark would never think to say to her, "Well, I only mocked you out." Thus, venial sin is something to be concerned about; all infidelity to love is something to be concerned about. Our goal is union with the Father; our direction should be one of getting closer and closer to him.

162 YOUR FAITH AND YOU

What are some examples of venial sin? Failing to pray is a definite sign of lack of growth. The reason for this is that communication is essential for any relationship. This is a good example of where sin can be an *omission*. Another example of venial sin is cheating on an examination. Here is an act of *commission* where a person has taken something of value which does not belong to him or her. Like all sin, cheating has social consequences. Others are affected by what I do. In this example, the sinner affects not only himself, but the other students, the teachers, and perhaps all other people he or she will ever contact in the future. Why will it tend to affect others outside of those immediately hurt by the sin? Simply put, because sin tends to make us "stiff-necked," "hard-hearted," and "stubborn," thus affecting all our relationships (Is 29:13; Jer 5:23). Cheating, then, weakens the love relationship between the Father and the sinner because it weakens the love relationship between the sinner and others with whom Jesus identifies himself (Mt 25:31-46).

*Mortal sin* (c) is the harboring of a serious attitude or the commission of some serious action that kills the relationship of love between the Father and the sinner. The Father's love is always there; he does not kill the relationship. Rather, the sinner kills the relationship by completely turning his or her back on God's love and saying "no" to the relationship. Knowing the nature of love and being in a loving relationship, we know that it is not easy to commit a mortal sin. But saying it is difficult is not to say it is impossible. Three conditions must be met, though: (1) *The action or attitude itself must be serious*. Murder, for example, is serious because it is obvious to see how a relationship is killed when another person is eliminated. Adultery, too, is a serious breach of covenant love within a marriage. Rape seriously exploits another person. Attitudes of deep hatred towards minority groups are often fatally destructive of love between peoples and often lead to violence. (2) A person must *know* the action is sinful. One is not blameworthy for something one does not know. However, we have a continual obligation to learn, to clear up ignorances, and grow in love (and knowledge) of the Lord. (3) One must *freely consent* to the evil. Modern psychology tells us there are a number of forces and drives that limit our freedom; for example, overwhelming fear might keep me from helping a dying person on the street (serious matter). Again, however, humans do have some freedom and are capable of serious wrongdoing. The testimony to that is the violence, hatred, callousness, neglect and the like so prevalent in the world today.

The diagram includes a final position, position *d*. This represents what has been traditionally called the state of mortal sin. After one has killed the relationship, the sinner has turned his or her back on God's love and is no longer in relationship. To correct this situation, the sinner must repent, that is, turn back to the Father, admit his or her wrongdoing and need for forgiveness. The Catholic has the privilege of receiving the sacrament of reconciliation where God's healing love is presented to us in a sign which reassures us of this love. The point of Jesus' parable of the Prodigal Son is precisely that no matter what we do or how often we do it, the Father's love is always there ready for us. We need but turn to him and accept his love. Ours is a God who is not out "to get us" the minute we slip up and step out of the relationship. Ours is a God who "got us," who continuously loves, who lets his light shine on the good man and the evil man. In essence, Christian morality is saying "yes" to this love, letting it shine on us, and then living a life of light which shines out to others so that in us others will see a child of God, a brother to our Savior and friend Jesus.

---

**EXERCISE:**

Below are listed several actions or attitudes which help weaken or destroy the love relationship between God and us. Individually try to (1) identify which of these are *serious matters* ( √ ) and (2) give a reason why these lessen or kill the love relationship. Then, discuss these as a class and with your teacher.

*Reason*

——  1. Fornication
(that is, premarital
intercourse)                    ——————————————

——  2. Not helping the poor   ——————————————

——— 3. Cussing (using
        gutter language)          _____

——— 4. Cursing (swearing)      _____

——— 5. Mocking out a class-
        mate                      _____

——— 6. Refusing to befriend
        a lonely classmate       _____

——— 7. Lying                    _____

——— 8. Disobeying a parental
        wish                      _____

——— 9. Abortion                 _____

——— 10. Getting drunk           _____


## WHAT DOES THIS MEAN?

The moral teaching of the Catholic Church is unlike many philosophical systems competing for the attention of young people today. Unlike the ethical system, atheistic communism, which denies the worth of the individual, Christian morality affirms the individual. You are unique. There is no one who can ever do in the world what you can do. As a person made in the image of God, you have special talents and abilities that no one else has. To the God who made you and to his Son Jesus, you are more valuable than the rarest gem. You are challenged to use your talents to serve others, to live out your vocation as children of God in a loving, creative way. As one person has put it: "What you are is God's gift to you, what you make yourself is your gift to God."

Second, our moral teaching respects our freedom. It recognizes that to coerce is antihuman. Central in our teaching is the role of conscience. Without a doubt, personal conscience is supreme in the making of moral decisions. We are invited to use it and continually to inform it so that it might be ever more sensitive to God and our fellow humans.

Third, Christian morality is rooted not in some ethical system but in our risen Lord and response to the Spirit. We do not have to learn abstract logical propositions to be good people. We have the example of Jesus who lives in his Church and in us believers. Ultimately, our norm for judging whether we are doing right or wrong is the question, "What would Jesus have done?"

Finally, Christian morality is an invitation—an invitation to say yes to our vocation as children of God, a yes to God's law of love. This is a tremendous dignity. Christian morality is at its core realistic. It is realistic in that it recognizes that we should be optimistic because our Lord has won for us our redemption. Christians have faith that they can, with our Lord's help, be true to their call. But it is also realistic in noting that there is sin in the world, and that we need the guidance of law and others on our journey together to the Father.

Young people are especially sensitive to a Church which respects their individuality and their freedom and in a realistic way challenges them to be everything they were ever called to be.

OTHER QUESTIONS:

Perhaps more than any other question, the following is most often asked by young people concerning Christian morality.

> Isn't the Church, in this day and age, somewhat out
> of date in its teaching on sexual morality? In fact,
> isn't its teaching too restrictive?

It is certainly understandable why young people (and others, as well) ask this question. Ours is an age which tolerates all kinds of behavior in the area of sexual morals. Song lyrics, advertisements, movies, prime-time T.V. shows, magazines, and the like, extol sexual practices which an older generation felt were better reserved only for certain times and places and only between married people.

We in the Catholic community still feel it is right to praise the virtues of married love not because we are prudish but because we believe in the sacredness of sex and sexual love. For example, concerning premarital sex, we teach the virtue of chastity because of our tremendous respect for our share in God's creative activity. So often sex is used to exploit others or is indulged in for selfish motives or under the guise of love. Sexual intercourse and all acts leading up to it are reserved for committed married love not because sex is bad. Rather, sex is so good that it is a share in bringing the mystery of new life into being. Sexual love should only be manifested when two people have given their lives to each other totally and with no strings attached (marriage). The act itself signifies a total giving and a total receiving. To do it outside of the total giving and receiving of marriage is to make a mockery of the symbol.

However, the Church realizes the pressures young people face today. It offers its help, its prayers, its encouragement and its love to all young people who face the difficult struggle of living chastely in a world satiated with false sexual values. It challenges all people to live virtuously in the area of sex in order to respect themselves and others. Failures in the area of sexual morality should never be occasions of self-hatred but rather examples of our own weakness and need for continual conversion. We should always remember the good news of God's infinite love for us and his acceptance of us in our weakness.

SUMMARY

The following are offered as brief summary points of this chapter.

1. Christian morality is responsibility, that is, a *response* to God's call of love and the *ability* freely given to respond in love.

2. Christian morality is, at its heart, covenantal and as a result demands fidelity to our vocation as children of God.

3. The Ten Commandments and the Beatitudes are excellent standards to measure the quality of Christian response to God and to neighbor.

4. Conscience is the subjective norm of morality which helps one choose right and wrong. Conscience must be followed and continually formed.

5. Law is an objective norm of morality which helps guide the conscience.

6. Jesus is our ultimate and absolute norm.

7. Sin is ultimately a failure in covenant love. It can either weaken or kill a living relationship with God and neighbor.

## EVALUATION

In light of what you read and studied in this chapter, please go back to the opening exercises and answer once again Tom Johnson's dilemma. If you changed any of your reasons or your choice as to what he should do, try to state why.

---

**EXERCISE:**

On a given day, bring your local newspaper to class. Select three (3) news articles and one or two editorials. As a class read these and then critique what took place or what is commented on in light of Christian morality. Concerning the editorial, if your class finds that you disagree with the view(s) taken, compose a letter and send it to the editor espousing the Christian values you stand for. You might critique a given television show in the same way and send letters to state your views.

---

# 7

# Church in the Modern World

*"Anyone among you who aspires to greatness must serve the rest, and whoever wants to rank first among you must serve the needs of all. Such is the case with the Son of Man who has come, not to be served by others, but to serve, to give his own life as a ransom for the many."*

(Mt 20:26-28)

At its very core, the Church is missionary. A missionary is one who is sent to carry out a specific task. The Church derives its mandate from Jesus himself who, on Easter Sunday, instructed his apostles, "As the Father has sent me, so I send you" (Jn 20:21). What is the specific task of the Church? In reality, it is threefold: to be the herald, the sign, and the servant of the Gospel. The Church fulfills its role as herald when it teaches and proclaims the truth of Christ's Gospel. As a sign of the Gospel, the Church has the task to live the truth of the good news in a community of believers. Lastly, as servant of the Gospel, the Church has a social mission. The Church fulfills its social mission when it witnesses to the message of God's saving love for the world. It does this best when it manifests God's love by ministering to people in need.

A criticism of the Church has been that in its concern for "getting people to heaven," it neglects this world and the people who are suffering in it. Karl Marx in particular claimed that the Church was "an opiate of the people" which drugged them with promises of "pie in the sky bye and bye," but was too little concerned with their plight of suffering in the world. It would be unfair to say that there was no truth in Marx's critique. As a matter of fact, churchmen sometimes did neglect the social dimension of the Gospel, while preaching to the poor and oppressed a quiet acceptance of their situation in life. This often happened when they allied themselves too closely with particular forms of governments in power (the status quo) which all too often were reluctant to better the lot of the poor. Or it sometimes resulted from a false dualism that held that things of this world (material reality) were of little concern to mankind which was destined for a supernatural world (spiritual reality). This dualism held that spiritual reality has little to do with material reality.

Regardless of the neglect of some church people, however, it has been the constant teaching of the Church that work for justice has been an essential ingredient in the ministry of the Church. This truth has been strongly reaffirmed in our day in a document from the synod (a worldwide meeting) of bishops entitled *Justice in the World* (1971). This document holds that working for justice in the world ranks with the celebration of the sacraments and the preaching of the Gospel as essential ministries in the Church. Home and foreign missions, disaster relief agencies, hospitals and medical clinics, orphanages, programs for young people, services for the elderly and the apostolate of education are just a few of the programs through which the Church has witnessed to justice in the past and continues to witness in the present.

The present chapter will summarize briefly some of the highlights in the social teaching of the Church. The organization of the chapter will be a bit different than previous chapters. Presented below is a short pretest which aims to examine your present knowledge of the Church's social teaching. The rest of the chapter, then, is designed to comment briefly on each item in the pretest.

## PRETEST ON SOCIAL JUSTICE

*Directions:* Mark each item on the test either "true" or "false" based on your current understanding of Catholic Church teaching on social justice. Correct your test by referring to answers given on p. 174 and then compare yourself to the evaluatory responses at the end of this section.

———— 1. The social teaching of the Church is rooted in the dignity of human beings.

———— 2. We work out our salvation in isolation from others.

———— 3. A starving child in India has a real relationship to the secure person in the United States of America.

———— 4. Human rights have to be earned by people before they should be granted to them.

———— 5. Rights exist independent of duties.

———— 6. You can have love without justice but you cannot have justice without love.

———— 7. *Gaudium et Spes (The Church in the Modern World)* is the key Vatican II document on social justice.

———— 8. The family in its life-giving and love-sharing serves as a model for the larger societies.

———— 9. The national government has a unique role in promoting the common good.

———— 10. The Church generally holds that the larger society should always take over functions normally handled by smaller units in society.

———— 11. The Church would support women's liberation up to where sex differences would be denied or family life would be eroded.

———— 12. Because law rarely changes people's attitudes, it should not be used to improve discriminatory practices until attitudes are changed some other way.

———— 13. The Catholic Church does not support the so-called right of workers to unionize.

———— 14. If people have the financial resources, they should be allowed to live where they wish to live.

———— 15. There is little the individual can do to foster social justice in society as a whole.

———— 16. The Christian has little hope that the problems in the international sphere can ever be solved.

———— 17. Rich nations should be taxed in order to help the poorer nations to develop.

———— 18. The United Nations should be disbanded.

———— 19. It is easy to justify war in the modern day.

———— 20. In every circumstance the Christian should be against all war.

*Evaluation of Pretest* (Answers on p. 174)

| | |
|---|---|
| 18-20 correct: | an excellent grasp of Church teaching in the area of human rights. |
| 15-17 correct: | a better than average knowledge of Church teaching on justice. |
| below 15 correct: | be sure to carefully read the rest of the chapter to learn about the Church's progressive ideas in the area of justice and development. |
| *Bonus question:* | List three important Church documents in the area of human rights and justice. |

a. _____

b. _____

c. _____

## KEY IDEAS AND TERMS

*Dignity of the person* (Q-1). The social teaching of the Catholic Church rests on the dignity of the human person. Our basic dignity flows from our being made to the image of God with a capability of knowing and loving our Creator. We have been appointed by God as master of all earthly creatures so that we might subdue them and use them to God's glory (*Church in the Modern World,* 12). As the Psalmist puts it:

> What is man that you should be mindful of him;
>     or the son of man that you should care for him?
> You have made him less than the angels,
>     and crowned him with glory and honor.
>
> (Ps 8:5-6)

*People by nature are social* (Q-2). Though we are the crown of creation, we are not isolated beings made separate from one another. From the beginning, God created us for companionship, "male and female he created them" (Gn 1:27). By our very natures we are social beings who need to relate to others both in order to live and to develop our potential. The three communities to which we belong and which are most often discussed in papal social teaching are illustrated below in the form of concentric circles. We cannot help but relate to all three communities because we belong to all three.

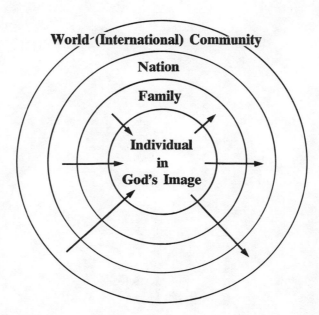

*The goal of human solidarity* (Q-3). Because we are social and communal beings, we live in a network of human relationships which affects us as individuals. Likewise, we have an impact on others. We cannot escape our call to unity, that is, solidarity, which is so well exemplified in Jesus' prayer to his father,

> "that all may be one
> as you, Father, are in me, and I in you."
> 
> (Jn 17:21)

---

*Answers to Pretest:*

| | | | | |
|---|---|---|---|---|
| 1. True | 5. False | 9. True | 13. False | 17. True |
| 2. False | 6. False | 10. False | 14. True | 18. False |
| 3. True | 7. True | 11. True | 15. False | 19. False |
| 4. False | 8. True | 12. False | 16. False | 20. False |

---

Thus, what happens to one person affects the unity of all. When one person suffers, I suffer because I am related to that person. Besides, as we have seen, each person has dignity resulting from being made in God's image and likeness. Every person is basically equal, enjoying the same divine calling and destiny. As the document on *The Church in the Modern World* puts it:

> True, all men are not alike from the point of view of varying physical power and the diversity of intellectual and moral resources. Nevertheless, with respect to the fundamental rights of the person, every type of discrimination, whether social or cultural, whether based on sex, race, color, social condition, language, or religion, is to be overcome and eradicated as contrary to God's intent (29).

*Rights and duties* (Q-4). The dignity of a person is protected by rights which are moral claims a person can make on other persons and on society in general. Below are listed a number of human rights discussed and defended in a number of Church documents as flowing from the very dignity of the human person. Some of these will be discussed in more detail later in the chapter.

*Economic rights*
— right to work
— right to a just wage
— right to property

*Political rights*
— right to participate in governments
— right to judicial protection

*Cultural rights*
— right to education
— right to freedom of speech

*Social rights*
— right to assembly
— right of free association

*Religious rights*
— right to worship

*Other rights*
— right to emigrate/ immigrate
— right to development

Every right has a corresponding duty for others to respect, foster and fulfill the right. Furthermore, the person has a duty corresponding to his or her right. For example, the right to a just wage dictates the duty to an honest day's work for the pay given. The right to participate in one's government carries with it the duty to vote in elections. Or, finally, the right of freedom of speech demands honesty and kindness in exercising it (Q-5).

*Social justice and Gospel love* (Q-6). Social justice refers to that part of Church teaching and Christian life which attempts to apply the Gospel command of love to the structures, systems and institutions of society. It is in these structures, systems and institutions where all human relationships (personal, political, economic, cultural) take place. What is the relationship between justice and love? Simply put, as stated in *Justice in the World,* "love implies an absolute demand for justice, usually a recognition of the dignity and rights of one's neighbor." I cannot say I love a person if I do not in justice respect and respond to the rights and basic needs of my neighbor. St. John states this relationship beautifully:

If anyone says, "My love is fixed on God,"
yet hates his brother,
he is a liar.
One who has no love for the brother he has seen
cannot love the God he has not seen.
The commandment we have from him is this:
whoever loves God must also love his brother.
(1 Jn 4:20-21)

Love means giving of self to others. It is impossible to love without *sharing* with others what is due them by right (justice). Love can go beyond justice, however, in going the extra mile in the service of others, that is, in imitating the love of Jesus. To state this another way, in a sense, justice is simply the minimal human and Christian response to others. Love, if we are serious about becoming like Christ, requires going beyond justice, that is, beyond what is simply due a person.

*Social Documents of the Church:* Below are listed some of the key Church documents which treat social justice. Papal encyclicals are important letters addressed to Catholics (and often other Christians and men and women of good will). They represent the ordinary teaching of the Church which is an excellent guide for Catholics in the formation of their consciences. Papal addresses and letters from groups of bishops also reiterate significant Church teaching. A council document (like *Gaudium et Spes*) is highly authoritative writing.

| LATIN NAME FOR ENCYCLICAL OR DOCUMENT | YEAR | ENGLISH TRANSLATION | AUTHOR | TOPIC(S) TREATED |
|---|---|---|---|---|
| *Rerum Novarum* . . papal encyclical | 1891 | *Of New Things* | Pope Leo XIII | Discusses unjust wage system in an economy |
| *Quadragesimo Anno* . . papal encyclical | 1931 | *On the Fortieth Anniversary of Rerum Novarum* | Pope Pius XI | In light of Gospel, treats rights and duties of capital and labor. |
| ——— | 1940-1957 | Christmas addresses of Pope Pius XII | Pope Pius XII | On various social issues |
| *Mater et Magistra* . . papal encyclical | 1961 | *Mother and Teacher* | Pope John XXIII | Discusses the rights and duties involved in the economic growth and development within a country |
| *Pacem in Terris* . . papal encyclical | 1963 | *Peace on Earth* | Pope John XXIII | Treats responsibilities of rich nations toward poor nations, the urgency of nuclear disarmament, and racial discrimination |
| *Gaudium et Spes* . . Vatican II Council Document (Q-7) | 1965 | *Pastoral Constitution on the Church in the Modern World* | Pope Paul VI & Council fathers | A key Council document discussing the Church's mission to the contemporary world |
| *Populorum Progressio* . . papal encyclical | 1967 | *On the Development of Peoples* | Pope Paul VI | Discusses the structures of international economic systems |

| | | | | |
|---|---|---|---|---|
| *Octogesima Adveniens* | 1971 | *On the Occasion of the Eightieth Anniversary of Rerum Novarum* | Pope Paul VI | Discusses recent patterns of socio-economic organization and sounds a call to action on them |
| *Justitia in Mundo . . the synod of Bishops* | 1971 | *Justice in the World* | Second Synod of Bishops | Critiques inter-national economic systems especially in the light of *Populorum Progressio* |
| ——— | 1976 | *To Live in Christ Jesus* | Ameri-can Con-ference of Catho-lic Bishops | Discusses principles of moral life and applies them to the family, nation and community of nations |

---

For Discussion:

1. Study as a group or individuals one or more of these documents. Your teacher can point out some of the more important sections of the documents. Report your findings to the class.

2. Analyze one day of your life. List all the people who affect you and whom you affect. Discuss John Donne's famous saying "No man is an island." Does it apply to you?

3. What is the meaning of respect? For whom do you have the most respect? Why? Is someone entitled to our respect even if: a. they have no self-respect? or b. they do not respect us? Why or why not?

4. Make a list of student rights and corresponding duties. Are each of these a matter of justice or love or both?

---

## SOCIAL TEACHING AND FAMILY LIFE

The bedrock unit of any society is the family. Its special value often lies in its willingness to affirm and to love individuals not for what they accomplish or the possessions they own but simply for who they are. Married couples in a Christian, sacramental union are to be a model of Christ's own love for the Church. His love is enduring and self-giving. "Husbands, love your wives, as Christ loved the church. He gave himself up for her . . ." (Eph 5:25).

*Children* (Q-8). Children are the greatest gift of marriage. They enrich the lives of their parents in many ways. Parents cooperate with the love of God the Creator when they regard as their proper mission the transmitting of human life and the education of their children (*Gaudium et Spes,* 50). Of course, parents have the right to choose responsibly the number of children they have, but selfishness can never be the determining factor. Thus, marriage is both love-sharing between the couple and life-giving. The twin values of life and love are a strong basis for the wider society.

*The Aged.* Our old are often neglected. In justice and in love, the elderly should be respected for their wisdom, their knowledge and experience. When possible, they should be welcomed into their own families. Christian families especially have an obligation to keep in touch with their aging parents and to care for them as best as possible. "If anyone does not provide for his own relatives and especially for his immediate family, he has denied the faith" (1 Tim 5:8). Society, furthermore, has an obligation to care for the aged who cannot take care of themselves.

---

For Reflection:

1. When was the last time you visited, called or wrote a grandparent?

2. Visit an old folks' home. Bring papers, magazines and the like to read to them. Talk to them. Do this on a regular basis.

---

## SOCIAL TEACHING AND THE NATION

Two themes dominate Church teaching as it applies to larger societies, namely, the *common good* and the *principle of subsidiarity*.

*Common good* (Q-9). The common good can be defined as all the spiritual, social and material conditions needed in society for the individual to achieve full human dignity. It is "the sum of those conditions of social life which allow not only groups but also their individual members to achieve their own fulfillment more fully and more readily" than they could on their own (*Gaudium et Spes,* 26). The whole society including individuals, organizations, public authorities and the like works for the common good, but the state has a unique role in achieving it first by preserving public order, and, as a last resort, intervening to bring about justice.

*The principle of subsidiarity* (Q-10). This principle holds that decisions should be made at the lowest reasonable level in order to enlarge freedom and to broaden participation in responsible action. Only when an individual or small unit cannot properly fulfill a task should the task be absorbed by the larger society. For example, parents have the *primary* responsibility of caring for their children. But, perhaps, there are some very good reasons parents cannot adequately take care of their children because of some extraordinary circumstances like the costly care of severely retarded children. Then, the larger society should step in and offer its help.

---

Below are listed a number of concerns, issues, problems and rights which the nation should be concerned about. These are more fully discussed in the American Bishops' document entitled *To Live in Christ Jesus* (1976).

*Respect for the unborn.* Jesus taught in the strongest of terms the need to care for the weak and the helpless in a special way. Unfortunately and tragically, in too many lands, innocent human life with great potential is snuffed out without ever seeing the light of day. For the sake of the common good, this right to life must be first recognized and then protected by the law. Furthermore, society needs to offer help and assistance to those women who feel that the only way out of their current problem is abortion. The Church, especially because of its pro-life witness, should be in the forefront in supporting women with problems during or after pregnancy, and thus bear strong witness to its belief in human dignity. Organizations like Birthright are one of today's means for fulfilling this responsibility.

*Women in society* (Q-11). Jesus himself recognized the equality and dignity of women. For example, his free association with women in public on a par with men often upset the expectations of the establishment of his day. The Church recognizes as praiseworthy and good those efforts which win recognition that women have the same dignity and fundamental rights as men. However, the Church cautions against views which would ignore or deny significant differences between the sexes, undermine marriage or motherhood, and erode family life and the basis of society itself.

*Respect for racial and ethnic groups* (Q-12). All racial and ethnic groups are beings of incomparable worth, because of their dignity as humans. Yet, individuals and the structures of society often discriminate to the disadvantage of innocent people. It is true that laws may not be able to change attitudes of prejudiced people, but they can foster justice by protecting minority groups, by deterring those who might otherwise violate the rights of others, and by educating people to know right from wrong. Racial justice must be fostered in nations especially in regard to housing, education, health care, employment and the administration of justice. In our country, racial injustice is a major problem. Concerned Christians will take positive steps to become aware of the issues involved. Furthermore, they will try to understand the causes of the problems, trying to see the consequences of various solutions. Lastly, they will do their part in trying to work for positive ways to foster the brotherhood of all peoples.

*Employment* (Q-13). The Church has spoken loudly and clearly on the rights of workers:

> Every man has the right to work, to a chance to develop his qualities and his personality in the exercise of his profession, to equitable remuneration which will enable him and his family "to lead a worthy life on the material, social, cultural and spiritual level" and to assistance in case of need arising from sickness or age.
>
> *(Octogesima Adveniens, 14)*

In addition, the Church recognizes the right of workers to organize (unionize). The Church cautions that certain abuses can result from strikes, for example, in overburdening the overall economy or unreasonably shutting down vitally needed public services.

*Housing* (Q-14). Individuals should be able to live where they wish and their means allow. Out of place are policies of governments, banks and the real estate industry which deprive certain racial, religious or ethnic groups of the necessary financing for housing.

## OTHER NATIONAL PROBLEMS

*Crime and criminals.* People have the right and need to live in peace and to be protected from criminals. Societies should work not only at stricter law enforcement but should also strive to root out the sources of much crime—poverty and injustice, as well as society's compulsion for individuals to acquire material possessions in order to be worthwhile. Prisoners, too, have rights: they have the right to protection from assault, a right to proper food, health care and recreation, and opportunities to pursue other human goals such as education.

*Migrant workers and prisoners of war. Justice in the World* especially laments the condition of migrant workers who are often the victims of discriminatory attitudes and are often obliged to live an insecure and inhuman life. Mentioned, too, are prisoners of war being treated in an inhuman manner.

*Communications.* Pope Paul VI calls for public authorities to carefully watch the growing power and influence of the media on social communications and indicates that the men who hold the power of the media have a "grave responsibility with respect to the truth of the information they spread, the needs and the reactions they generate and the values they put forward" (*Octogesima Adveniens,* 20).

*Environment.* Mankind has responsibility for the environment, too. We are suddenly becoming aware that in our ill-considered exploitation of nature, we risk destroying it and becoming victims of the destruction. Pollution, refuse, and new illnesses result from an unchecked technology, creating an environment which may be intolerable in the future. Responsibility demands careful planning, conservation, and an unselfish respect for the goods of this world.

---

Discussion and Reflection:

1. What do you think of the range of the Church's concern in its social teaching? Does this surprise you?

2. (Q-15). You might wonder after reading the above: "What can I as an individual do to further these rights of so many different groups?" The Church has traditionally offered the *corporal* and *spiritual* works of mercy as concrete steps the concerned, socially aware Christian can follow. Translate each of these into a concrete act of caring and sharing which a young person can realistically perform. For example, give drink to the thirsty might mean to give the drink of friendship to a lonely classmate who thirsts for companionship. Or visiting the imprisoned might mean going to a nursing home to visit an elderly invalid person. Choose one task from each list and resolve to do it in the upcoming week.

| CORPORAL WORKS OF MERCY | SPIRITUAL WORKS OF MERCY |
|---|---|
| 1. Feed the hungry. (concrete application) | 1. Convert the sinner. (concrete application) |
| 2. Give drink to the thirsty. | 2. Instruct the ignorant. |

| | |
|---|---|
| 3. Clothe the naked. | 3. Counsel the doubtful. |
| 4. Visit the imprisoned. | 4. Comfort the sorrowful. |
| 5. Shelter the homeless. | 5. Bear wrongs patiently. |
| 6. Visit the sick. | 6. Forgive all injuries. |
| 7. Bury the dead. | 7. Pray for the living and the dead. |

## SOCIAL TEACHING AND THE COMMUNITY OF NATIONS

The concern of the Christian for the rights of others does not stop with the family or with his or her own nation. Following the lead of Jesus who called upon his followers to love all people, even our enemies, the Christian in the modern world must show concern for the international community as well. Of course, not only Christian love and justice prompt us to extend our sense of care beyond our national borders. An intelligent and concerned person of Christian conscience will look at the scope of worldwide problems and their seriousness and conclude that it is foolish not to get involved in the furthering of the rights of all humans.

Problems which loom on the horizon and which make any concerned person conclude that the world is sick include:

- *hunger* (It is conservatively estimated that two people per minute die of starvation.)

- *environmental pollution* (Living in some of our cities is like smoking two packs of cigarettes daily.)

- *population growth and wastefulness* (Some social scientists claim the earth will deplete its resources within the next 50 years.)

- *glaring disparities of wealth* (The United States, for example, consumes around 35% of the world's marketable resources, yet has only 6% of the world's population.)

- *persistent danger of war* (The arms race has produced the capability to annihilate every man, woman and child living today more than a hundred times over.)

*Christian hope* (Q-16). These problems are enough to make the fainthearted prone to despair. But regardless of their seriousness, Christians are still fundamentally optimistic because we know that without Christ we can do nothing, but with Christ we can do all things. Our mission in the world focuses on what we can do, not on what we cannot do. Certainly what we can do is significantly more than we are doing now.

*Development of peoples.* Of major concern to Pope Paul VI in his recent writings is that nations be allowed to develop and become liberated (that is, free) from oppressive practices and situations which often keep the poorer nations in their dependent and often hopeless conditions. The pope points to the example of already developed nations and tries to show that if poor nations too can develop then several of the problems listed above can be improved. Development helps bring the kind of wealth which enables nations to have a better chance at self-sufficiency.

A constant theme in papal teaching concerning developing nations has been the right of developing nations and people to control and direct their own process of development, even though foreign money and technical assistance are also included in the process. Thus, the right to development includes both economic growth and political, social and economic participation in the process of development.

More concretely, what can rich nations do to help poor nations develop? In his famous encyclical *Populorum Progressio* (The Development of Peoples), Pope Paul VI outlines a four-point plan which will help distribute wealth among the nations and aid poor nations to develop without strong manipulation from the rich nations which may wish only to gain political favors.

1. *Charitable giving* (*Populorum Progressio,* 44-45). Private individuals and organizations as well as governments will always have the responsibility to aid those in need. CARE, the Bishops' Relief Fund, gifts to the missions and the like are examples of the kinds of things people have the obligation to support out of love and justice.

2. *Creation of a world fund* (51) (Q-17). The pope calls for the creation of a world bank to be supported by cutbacks of military expenditures in the developed nations. This world fund, which in effect is supported by a form of taxation on the rich nations, would be used to combat the poverty of the poor nations and aid them in development, for example, in efforts to industrialize.

3. *Rectifying trade relationships* (57-61). Pope Paul VI rightly recognized the disadvantages poor nations have on the world market. All too often, rich nations set the prices of the raw materials they import from the poor nations and on the manufactured goods they export back to the poor nations. This creates a grave imbalance for the poor nations. The pope strongly points out that the same standards worked out within the developed nations—like paying a just wage to workers and consumer protection laws—be rigidly applied outside their borders when dealing with poor nations. The resulting balance will at least give the poor nations a chance to develop.

4. *Creation and support of international organizations which will coordinate and direct a new judicial order* (78). The pope would support a United Nations with real *political* and *judicial* clout to help prevent the rich from exploiting the poor and aid the poor in their development (Q-18).

Discussion and Activity:

1. What do you think of Pope Paul VI's teaching? Is it realistic?

2. What would you add to his list?

3. Carrying out the social aspect of the gospel is rarely easy. It often involves great courage, clear thinking and decisive action in prayerful fidelity to the gospel. It also involves a respectful yet forceful dialogue with those forces opposing the Christian social value in question. The following statements are intended to help sensitize the class to the art of dialogue which is often called for in striving for Christian social justice. Listed below are a number of positions on different issues which, for one reason or another, are opposed to the gospel. Respond as a class to each position.

Prison reform: By their crimes, those in prison have surrendered all claims to be treated like human beings. Besides, the rehabilitation of the criminal is too costly as it is.

Christian principle threatened in this position

_____

A possible Christian position on this issue _____

_____

Abortion: The rights of the mother are the only thing that matters here. The mother's rights to life, liberty and the pursuit of happiness must not be hampered by an unwanted baby.

Christian principle threatened in this position

_____

A possible Christian position on this issue _____

_____

World Hunger: American eating habits are of no concern to other nations. Nor are we bound to sacrifice our American standard of living to help people we do not even know. Let them solve their own problems.

Christian principle threatened in this position

A possible Christian position on this issue_____

_____

Drug Addiction: Everyone has to live his own life. If someone wants to take the risk of ruining it that is his or her business.

Christian principle threatened in this position

A possible Christian position on this issue_____

_____

*Peace* (Q-19-20). In recent years, the Church has deplored the arms race not only because it fosters a balance of terror but because the tremendous financial resources used to develop more destructive weapons could be used more productively. The Church is more and more beginning to question whether modern war can ever be justified to maintain peace. In both its execution and its technology modern war results in such savagery that all-out war would destroy humanity. The almost inevitable involvement of innocent noncombatants and the long-range environmental effects make modern thermonuclear war highly condemnable.

This is not to say that the Catholic Church has denied nations the right to self-defense. On the contrary, the Church has allowed the just war of defense under certain very specific conditions:

1. Vital rights of the nation, like its sovereign independence, are unjustly violated.

2. Other means of preventing the aggression of the unjust attacker have been tried but have failed (means like embargoes, diplomacy, economic sanctions).

3. There is a proportion between the foreseen evil effects of the war and any good that might come from it. Thus, a war resulting in more evil than good could not be allowed.

Nations should do all they can to prevent war. Furthermore, they should respect the right of individuals to object conscientiously to war in general and the right to object conscientiously to particular wars. The Church, in other words, allows the option of *Christian pacifism* while at the same time teaching the just-war theory.

True peace cannot be built on an aggression or terror but on the recognition of the rights of others and the performance of duties in respect to those rights both in justice and charity.

For Discussion:

1. Debate the morality of World War II and the Vietnam war using the "just-war theory." You will need to research the topic.

2. What is "Christian pacifism"? Do you admire pacifists? Why or why not?

## EVALUATION

Give three people the pretest which appears at the beginning of the chapter. At least one person should be an adult, another should be a peer. Either read the test to them or have copies made. Correct their exams and explain to them any questions they may have.

## SUMMARY

This chapter presented the highlights of the Church's social teaching which comes from the Gospel mandate to witness the message of God's love in society. Its social teaching is an essential ingredient in the ministry of the Church.

1. People by nature are social and have responsibilities to all others. Our essential equality comes from the fact that we are all made in the image of God.

2. The dignity of persons is protected by certain God-given rights. Each right has a corresponding duty.

3. Christian love implies an absolute demand for justice which is the recognition of the dignity and rights of another person.

4. The primary unit of society is the family. Love within a marriage should be life-giving.

5. Actions on the national level should be governed by the principle of subsidiarity and the common good.

6. The Church has spoken clearly for the rights of the unborn, for respect for the dignity of women, for the rights of ethnic and racial groups, for the workers, for criminals, and has admonished the controllers of social communications.

7. Christian concern for justice must extend beyond national borders. *Populorum Progressio* has outlined excellently the problems of underdeveloped nations and given some concrete guidelines on how rich nations can aid the development of the poorer nations.

8. Though the Church allows a just war, it teaches that war must be a last resort and cautions strongly against the thermonuclear war. In addition, the Church respects the conscience of the individual to witness against war and for peace as a pacifist.

---

**Further Topics for Reflection and Action:**

1. As a group or as individuals, take any one of the topics discussed in this chapter and do an in-depth research report on it.

2. Design a service project to meet the needs of one of the groups discussed in this chapter.

3. Critique editorials and essays (for example, in *Time* magazine) on social issues in light of Church social teaching.

---

# 8

# Prayer: Seeking Union With God

*At every opportunity pray in the Spirit, using prayers and petitions of every sort. Pray constantly and attentively for all in the holy company.*

(Eph 6:18)

This chapter is about Christian prayer. Our main concern will be that of presenting some practical guidelines and suggestions to aid a young adult Christian to grow in his or her life of prayer. No discussion of prayer would be complete without some reference to the Eucharist. In fact, in addition to being a sacrifice, the Eucharist is perfect Christian prayer, for in it Christ himself prays one with us to the Father. But since a whole chapter is devoted exclusively to the Eucharist we will here reserve our reflections to private prayer.

Why People Pray

In this opening exercise give priority to the following eight reasons why people pray. Do this in small groups and then share conclusions and reasons for your answers with the class. Perhaps the class as a whole can think of and discuss other reasons why people pray.

1. Because a teacher in a religion class said all have to begin class with a prayer

193

2. Because you want to thank God for all your loved ones

3. Because you are feeling lonely

4. Because you want to get the highest grade in the room on an important test

5. Because you want to express your love for God

6. Because you feel you need God's help in facing an important decision

7. Because a friend of yours is in serious trouble

8. Because God might punish us if we do not pray to him

We all know the difference between indifferent, casual chatter with a passing acquaintance, and open, intimate conversation with a friend. The value of the latter, on the other hand, though more demanding in that it calls for some kind of commitment on our part, adds an important and lasting dimension to our lives.

A similar point can be made about prayer. The above exercise helped bring out the basic fact that true prayer is never phony, forced or automatic. It can never be carelessly or indifferently performed. Prayer is our honest, sincere turning to God. It is both the expression of our love and our need for God and the time in which we open ourselves to a deeper awareness and appreciation of God's love for us. Surely then, genuine, sincere prayer is an indispensable part of Christian life.

Some Basic Aspects of Prayer

1. Listed below are six basic attitudes proper to prayer. Consider each of them briefly as a class and then do the following:

   a. Indicate the extent to which you agree or disagree with each statement.

   b. Indicate the ways to foster and strengthen the attitude being discussed.

   c. List some of the forces in each of us and in the society as a whole that make the attitude often difficult to achieve.

*Recalling God's presence.* Paul says that "in God we live and move and have our being." God is ever mindful of us and our needs. But we very easily forget him. Prayer should begin by pausing for a few brief moments to recall God's presence within and around us.

*Sincerity and honesty.* Nothing is hidden from God. He sees us and loves us just the way we are. In prayer, we must go to God as a child goes to its father with total trust. We must let our prayer be sincere and honest. And, we must avoid being phony with ourselves or God in prayer.

*Pray often.* Prayer is a habit. We cannot pray only when we are in serious trouble and still hope to discover the value and importance of prayer in our lives. Prayer, like friendship, develops slowly by the accumulation of daily encounters with God.

*Pray primarily out of love for God.* We should never pray solely because we want God to give us something. We should simply trust that God knows all our needs, and that if we sincerely give our lives to him, he will care for us always. Prayer, in other words, should never be prompted by selfish motives.

*Learn to listen.* Listening in prayer is as important as speaking. We should try to learn to hear God speaking to us in the silence of our own hearts. In a day filled with noise, prayer can serve as a kind of quiet oasis where we rest for a moment in silent openness to God.

*Recalling God's presence throughout the day.* Prayer is an expression of our whole life before God. It makes little sense to pray and then live the rest of the day as though God never existed. It is good to learn to recall God's presence throughout the day and for fleeting moments be aware of him in the midst of all our daily activities.

2.  Compare each of the aspects of prayer listed above to a corresponding aspect of friendship. In other words, how does friendship call upon us to listen, to be sincere always, etc? What does this comparison of prayer to friendship reveal to us about the nature of prayer?

3.  Imagine living in daily fidelity to prayer as outlined above. How does prayer have the power to change our lives?

## THE FORMS OF CHRISTIAN PRAYER

Two thousand years of Christian faith have given us some traditional forms of Christian prayer. Reflection on each of these ways of praying should offer us some helpful hints as we continue in our own efforts to grow in prayer.

---

"You can lead a horse to water but you can't make him drink." Apply this old saying to prayer. Why must true prayer be something we ourselves freely choose to do?

---

## PRAYING THE SCRIPTURES

Using the scriptures for prayer is one of the most ancient as well as most rewarding forms of prayer. All of the scripture is fruitful material for our use in prayer but the psalms and the writings of the New Testament have proven especially suitable as a basis for prayer.

Before beginning our prayer we should do our best to be in a relatively quiet place and to take a moment or two to recall God's presence both within us and in his word which we are about to read. As we begin to read the passage we have selected *we should read it as though the words are being spoken personally to us by God*. We should pause after each sentence to become fully aware of the text's meaning and relevance in our daily lives. It is better to read only a few verses and really pray them, allowing their message to take root in our hearts, than to try to read long passages and only half understand the meaning of the words. Sometimes it is helpful to find one brief line that can easily be remembered and then recall the chosen line throughout the day as a way of fostering a sense of God's presence in all we do.

---

To Do and Discuss:

1. The scriptures are also very conducive to group prayer. If you have not already done so, you might want to organize a classroom scripture service. If your parish has evening prayer, a group in the class can go and report on the experience to the class.

2.  There is a saying, "you are what you read." Apply this
to the reading of the scriptures as discussed above.

3.  *A Classroom Scripture Service.*

Given below are suggested guidelines for a classroom scripture service. Of course, the class should feel
free to revise the format of the service to meet class
needs.

First select a suitable theme. Three possible themes
with appropriate readings for each are given at the
end of this exercise. Any dictionary of the Bible will
provide suitable readings for practically any theme the
class might choose. Once a theme and readings are
selected the readers should make sure they are prepared
well before the service begins.

The room in which the service is to be held should
be made as suitable as possible for prayer: Enthroning
the Bible, candles, incense, banners and the like can
all contribute toward a prayerful atmosphere.

**Opening:**

Let the leader ask all to pause to recall the presence
of God before reciting the opening prayer (which can
be written in advance by a class member).

**First Reading:**

The psalm or other reading should be preceded
and/or followed or interspersed with a refrain either
sung or recited by the class. Read the psalm clearly
and slowly in an atmosphere of prayer. End with a
period of silence.

**Other Readings:**

The session proceeds by repeating the sequence
chosen for the first reading.

**Closing:**

The prayer session can end with the Our Father,
a hymn, a record, or a prayer by the leader.

Three suggested themes with appropriate psalms:

Love and trust in God.
Ps 42, 56, 62, 63, 139, 146

Prayers for God's help
Ps 57, 69, 70, 140, 141

Praise of God
Ps 103, 104, 147, 148-150

## VOCAL PRAYERS

When the disciples asked Jesus to teach them how to pray he taught them to say the Our Father (Mt 6:9-13). Because of its source, the Our Father has been the most important of all vocal prayers for Christians from Jesus' day to the present. But there are other very important vocal prayers as well: The Creed and the Hail Mary, for example, have a long and sacred tradition in the Church. Of course, the Mass is a vocal prayer which all Catholic Christians say in sincere thanksgiving for the eternal life given to us by Christ.

When saying any vocal prayers we should do our best to avoid having the prayers become "just words." We should, in other words, say our prayers only after pausing to recall God's presence and then making the intention of having our words truly express what is in our hearts. This is true not only of prescribed oral prayers but also with our own spontaneous vocal prayers in which we pray aloud to God.

---

Sometimes, close friends will tell each other little things that have happened to them or things which the other already knows. Yet the two find the words meaningful because they are ways of sharing their love for each other.

Compare this to our vocal prayers to God who already knows all the details of our daily lives much better than we do.

---

## THE ROSARY

The rosary is an important prayer in the Catholic tradition for several reasons: First, it uses the vocal prayers of the "Hail Mary," the "Our Father" and the "Glory Be." Second, Mary's role in Christian life is to lead us to Christ. All fifteen mysteries of the rosary are meditations on the main events of Jesus' life. Third, the rosary is a form of meditation. The words of the "Hail Mary" help keep our minds from wandering as we meditate on the events in Christ's life.

The mysteries of the rosary are divided into three groups. "Saying the rosary" is a term that usually refers to reciting the "Hail Mary" ten times (called saying a decade) for each of the five mysteries on which we meditate. The mysteries are:

*The Joyful Mysteries*

The Annunciation
The Visitation of Mary
   to Elizabeth
The Birth of Jesus
The Presentation of Jesus
   in the Temple
The Finding of Jesus in
   the Temple

*The Sorrowful Mysteries*

The Agony in the Garden
The Scourging at the Pillar
The Crowning with Thorns
The Carrying of the Cross
The Crucifixion

*The Glorious Mysteries*

The Resurrection of Jesus
The Ascension of Jesus into Heaven
The Descent of the Holy Spirit on the Apostles
The Assumption of Mary into Heaven
The Crowning of Mary as Queen of Heaven

---

**ACTIVITIES:**

1. The class can go through the mysteries explaining what they know about each and its importance in Christian life.

2. The class can recite a decade of the rosary together. Afterward there can be a discussion on the technique of using the words of the "Hail Mary" to help keep the mind focused on the mystery of the decade being recited.

---

## MEDITATION

Today a great number of young people are expressing an interest in eastern forms of meditation such as yoga, Zen and transcendental meditation. The Church has a long history of promoting the practice of meditation as a means of aiding the believer's growth in union with Christ. Christian meditation can be divided into two main types; namely, interior reflection and wordless awareness.

*Interior reflection.* The place of meditation should be relatively quiet. Some people find that an atmosphere of prayer can be enhanced by lighting a candle or burning incense. It is especially important to pause long enough to gain interior calm and to place one's self in God's presence. Then the subject of meditation should be recalled. This can be anything from some words of Jesus, a scene in the gospels, a psalm or any reality that helps us realize God's personal love for us. The chosen theme should be reflected upon in an attempt to sink to a deeper appreciation and understanding of God's presence in our daily life.

Sometimes it is helpful to interchange interior meditation with oral prayers and the praying of the scriptures. During meditation we can assume any posture we find helpful. Some prefer sitting cross-legged on the floor. Others prefer to sit in a chair, and still others, lying flat on their back. Wherever we choose to meditate, whatever posture we use or whatever the theme, we must always be patient. It takes time to develop the skills of meditation. But such time and effort are always well spent, and, if pursued long enough, will prove to be very rewarding.

*Wordless meditation.* Wordless meditation is also called *contemplation.* In contemplation there are neither words, thoughts nor feelings of God but rather a deep, subtle, indescribable awareness of God at a level deeper than words can express. Usually at first this form of prayer is not practiced deliberately but is rather something some people feel themselves drawn to in their practice of other forms of prayer.

In wordless meditation the mind must be very still and empty of thought, yet at the same time fully awake and alert. The choosing of a quiet place, the assuming of a restful posture and above all the simple turning to God for guidance are all helpful in attaining this state of mind—the wordless contemplation of God. Also helpful are the quiet gazing at a simple object such as a cross, candle or flower and the quiet repetition of a simple word or phrase such as "Jesus" or "God loves me." These help still the mind's constant flow of images.

When practicing this form of meditation it is advisable to have the guidance of a counselor, a priest, teacher or some adult who lives a life of prayer and whose opinion you can trust. It is good to keep in mind that this and all forms of prayer are not an end in themselves but only a means of deepening our union with Christ. Prayer should foster our awareness of the real needs of others and should help us in our daily effort to serve others.

---

**ACTIVITY:**

1. *A Sample Meditation*

   Meditate on a parable of Jesus. Select a favorite parable of Jesus which appeals to you. Before you pray, ask for God's help in this time of prayer. Take time to become relaxed and block out all distractions. Perhaps deep breathing will help. Assume a comfortable position.

   Read the parable and let it come to life for you. Take the following approach in meditating on the passage:

   a. Let the story become part of you and you become part of what is happening.

      (1) What is *really* going on here?

      (2) What is Jesus saying here?

      (3) What is Jesus like? What does he seem to be saying about God?

      (4) How does the story seem to affect others?

      (5) What does this story say to me? Am *I* a character in the story?

      (6) What is Jesus teaching *me* in this story?

   b. Take the whole theme of the passage (e.g., love of all men and women) and try to see all of the applications of it to your life right now.

   c. Now, turn your heart to God and respond to his presence in you. Share with him your feelings and thoughts. Share with him your needs, your gratitude, your praise, your sorrow over past failings. If you get distracted, you may wish to return to the Scripture passage. Take your time and enjoy these moments with the Lord.

*A List of Some Parables of Jesus*

Laborers in the Vineyard, Mt 20:1-16

Merciless Official, Mt 18:21-35

Rich Man and Lazarus, Lk 16:19-31

Good Samaritan, Lk 10:25-37

Good Shepherd, Jn 10:1-21

Prodigal Son, Lk 15:11-32

Treasure and the Pearl, Mt 13:44-46

Mustard Seed and the Leaven, Mk 4:30-32

2. Those who wish to do so may volunteer to practice some kind of daily prayer such as those suggested in this chapter. A daily journal should be kept of your honest reactions to this experience of prayer.

*The Jesus Prayer*. This prayer is a specific form of meditation which is becoming very popular among a growing number of Christians today. The prayer consists essentially of the constant repetition of the name of Jesus. The historical origins of this prayer go back to Jesus' own promise that "whatever you ask the Father in my name will be given to you" (Jn 16:23-24). By the sixth century the eastern rite church had developed a definite spirituality based on the calling upon Jesus' name.

In practicing the Jesus prayer one quietly repeats the words, "Lord Jesus Christ, Son of God, have mercy on me a sinner." Usually, however, a much briefer form is used, such as "My Jesus, mercy," or simply the word "Jesus." Also involved in the practice of the Jesus prayer is the linking up of one's breath and heartbeat with the words of the prayer. This is done by first spending a few moments breathing in and out in a slow, deep, relaxed manner. Then, each breath is accompanied by the words of the prayer.

Quietly or in your mind say, "Lord Jesus" as you breathe in, and "have mercy on me" as you breathe out. The traditional instructions for this form of prayer also place a great importance on the heart as well as the breath. As you breathe in saying "Lord Jesus" imagine that Jesus is breathed into your heart. As you exhale to the words "have mercy on me" imagine that you are exhaling from your heart all that separates you from Christ. Here, of course, the heart is a symbol of the center or source of our love for Jesus. The ultimate goal of this form of prayer is that of a gradual deepening of our love for Christ and the ability to enter into his presence by the simple calling out of his name.

---

What Do You Think?

1. Why is the Mass the most important shared prayer of Catholic Christians? What *attitudes* are needed in order for all present to fully enter into the reality of the Mass?

2. Do you think that our society today is such that many Christians feel awkward in expressing their faith before others, even with fellow Christians in times of shared prayer? Do you think this is good or bad?

3. Do you think the practice of prayer can be abused and made into a form of escape from the realities of daily life? How do you think this most often occurs? What are some remedies?

---

*Communal Prayer.* In recent years many Catholics have redis-covered the value of praying together. All forms of shared prayer express the vital truth that prayer is always communal, that is, that it always unites us and makes us one in Christ.

We already discussed a communal scripture service. But there are countless other ways of praying together as a group. Ideally every Christian family should spend some time, even only if at grace before meals, in sincere shared prayer together. But many parishes also have regular times of shared prayer in various forms. Your school may also have a regular prayer group or time set aside in which those who wish can come together for prayer.

## WHAT DOES THIS MEAN?

The first Christians were not simply faithful followers of a set of Christian moral principles. On the contrary, they were men and women whose lives had been completely renewed and trans-formed by a real relationship with the risen Jesus. Prayer was then and remains today a central means by which Christians experience the presence of Jesus living within us by his indwelling Spirit. In prayer, we personally, consciously commune with God and allow him to take an ever more important place in our lives.

Seen in this way, prayer is essential to Christian life. Although at times difficult, prayer offers each of us an indispensable source of life and strength. Without prayer, Catholic life quickly becomes a sterile, shallow set of rules and rituals. With prayer we can find in our faith the fullness of life promised to us by Christ.

## OTHER QUESTIONS

Today there is an obvious interest in eastern religions, par-ticularly in eastern meditation techniques of yoga and Zen. Besides these, the religious cults such as the Hare Krishna and Reverend Moon groups are both drawing large numbers of young people to their ranks. The question this raises is, what is the proper Catholic response to these movements?

First we must make the important distinction between meditation as a *mental technique* as contrasted to an expression of religious faith. Transcendental meditation, for example, is purely a mental technique for quieting the mind. One who practices it can be an atheist, a Hindu or a Catholic. In itself the technique has nothing to do with an individual's beliefs. Similarly, the techniques of yoga and Zen meditation, understood as methods of sitting, breathing and recollecting the mind, are also not expressions of religious faith, but simply centuries-old methods which silence the mind. It is true that these techniques are not necessarily bound up with any religious beliefs.

The intention with which they are used can vary greatly. For some they may be a means of relaxing before going to sleep. For others they can be a way of preparing for prayer. Numerous Catholic retreat houses offer "Yoga retreats" or teach Zen meditation methods. But these techniques are totally removed from the Buddhist or Hindu faiths. They are often used by Christians to help them develop a conscious faith relationship with Christ in prayer. Likewise, the Buddhist or Hindu uses these same techniques to enter into a deeper union with God as his own religion has taught him to believe in him.

In conclusion, the eastern religions should be respected by the Catholic but this must not lead to a watering down or confusion with faith in Christ as he lives in the Church. Once this is understood then some Catholics trying to live a life of meditation may well find the techniques used in eastern religions to be very helpful in their Christian prayer. What is sad is when this is done without an appreciation of the rich contemplative tradition within the Church.

## SUMMARY

The following points summarize the material covered in this chapter:

1. The Eucharist is the perfect Christian prayer for it achieves perfectly the goal of all prayer, which is union with God achieved through the power of Christ active through the Spirit who dwells in us.

2. In praying we must: put ourselves in the presence of God, be sincere, pray often, pray not for selfish reasons but in order to give ourselves to God, listen to God as well as speak to him, and gradually let our whole day become filled with little moments of remembering God.

3. There are many different ways to pray. Some of them are: praying the scriptures, vocal prayers, the rosary, meditation, the Jesus prayer, and communal or shared prayer.

4. Prayer is important in our lives because it is our free, conscious opening of ourselves to God in whom alone our life has ultimate meaning.

## EVALUATION

As a means of helping you "pull together" all that is covered in this chapter write a paragraph or two in response to this statement:

"To be a Christian one must be a man or woman of prayer."

**ADDITIONAL EXERCISES:**

1. Research the influence of contemplative spiritualities in the history of the Church: the desert Fathers of Egypt, the Benedictine, Cistercian, Carthusian, Carmelite, and Camaldolese religious orders, the writings of St. Teresa of Avila, St. John of the Cross, St. Francis de Sales. The writings of contemporary authors such as

Thomas Merton, Charles de Foucauld, Anthony Bloom and Henri Nouwen are all possible sources.

2. The Hasidic movement in Judaism, the Sufi movement in Islam, the Yoga movement of Hinduism and the Zen movement of Buddhism are all movements in other world religions which emphasize prayer and meditation. Any one of them can be researched and the comparisons and contrasts to Christianity noted.

# 9

# Worshipping God: The Eucharist

> *"Let me solemnly assure you,*
> *if you do not eat the flesh of the Son of Man*
> *and drink his blood*
> *you have no life in you.*
> *He who feeds on my flesh*
> *and drinks my blood*
> *has life eternal,*
> *and I will raise him up on the last day."*
>
> (Jn 6:53-54)

A Christian is more than just a member of a Church that shares the common vision of the gospel among its members. He is more than one who works for the cause of Christ. The Christian belongs to a people who worship together. In its most general sense, Christian worship is our human response to God's gift of his Son Jesus. Worship includes a number of elements; for example, embodying the good news of Jesus in community, witnessing actively to God's saving love, but more obviously, the *liturgical* life of the Church.

The word "liturgy" is derived from the Greek word meaning the "people's work" or, more specifically, "the work of the people of God." Liturgy includes a number of activities like the sacraments, the Divine Office, Benedictions and novenas, official blessings of the Church and the like. But the best expression of the Church's worship of the Father is the holy sacrifice of the Mass, the Eucharist. It is the source and summit of the Church's life and power (*Con-*

209

*stitution on the Sacred Liturgy,* 9). This entire chapter will be devoted to the theology of the Eucharist because of its central role in the life of a Catholic.

**EXERCISE:**

Before we discuss the theology of the Eucharist, please complete the following questionnaire.

*Part 1:*   Fill in the following information.

a. My favorite sport: _____

b. My best teacher: _____

c. The person I most respect: _____

d. The best music I've ever heard: _____

e. My favorite place: _____

f. A close friend: _____

*Part 2:*   Friendship

Arrange in order of importance the following qualities you think will help friendship grow.

1. ——   a. Talking to a friend
2. ——   b. Listening to a friend
3. ——   c. Being willing to accept a friend no matter what
4. ——   d. Spending time with a friend
5. ——   e. Understanding the problems of a friend
6. ——   f. Always being available to a friend
7. ——   g. Praising a friend for his or her good qualities

*Part 3:*   Discussion

1. Share some of the responses from Part 1 with your classmates. Oftentimes a reflection on the "good things in life" prompts thanksgiving to God for sending us so many blessings. Eucharist means "thanksgiving." Perhaps you and your classmates can together compose a prayer of thanksgiving which could be used after reception of holy communion at a class Mass.

2. In small groups, share individual rankings from Part 2. For each part, give a concrete experience from your own friendships. How is the Mass an opportunity to grow in friendship with our Lord Jesus?

## KEY TEACHINGS

The Eucharist is the sublime means of thanking God the Father for the gift of his Son, Jesus Christ. In addition, like all the sacraments, it is a mystery, the depths of which we can never totally fathom. But, nevertheless, there are several aspects to the Eucharist which we will discuss in order to help shed some light on the mystery.

The following illustration demonstrates five aspects of the Eucharist. Each one in turn will be discussed in this section of the chapter.

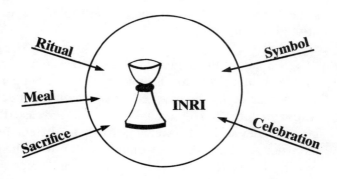

1. *Eucharist as Symbol.* The Eucharist, like all the sacraments, is a special kind of symbol. It is an outward sign instituted by Jesus Christ which symbolizes what it brings about and brings about what it symbolizes.* Within the Eucharistic action itself, there are a number of special symbols which help carry some of the profound meaning of the sacrament.

* For a discussion of symbols, see chapter V, "The Sacraments—Living Encounters with Christ."

a. *Word*. The symbol of the word is used in various Scripture readings, prayers, responses and the like. It is a powerful symbol because it conveys God to us, thus, the term, "the word of God." Reflect on ordinary human words. In a very real sense, they enable us to be human; without them, we would be like the animals and unable to transmit culture. Just as ordinary human words make us human, the word of God in the Eucharist helps to form us as his children. And especially when we hear the word and respond to it, then we are truly transformed.

b. *Bread*. Bread is the symbol of life. It is the ordinary food of vast numbers of humans. Without it, we would die. Consecrated bread at the Eucharist is life itself, namely, Jesus Christ. Without him we are spiritually dead.

We use *unleavened* bread in the Mass for three reasons: First, Jesus used it when he instituted the Eucharist at the Last Supper.

Second, in the context of the Passover meal that Jesus was celebrating with his disciples at the Last Supper, it was a reminder of the unleavened bread the ancient Jews had to use in the Sinai desert. They used "unyeasted" bread because they did not have time for it to rise for fear that the troops of the Pharaoh would catch up with them while it was rising. The Jews used unleavened bread in their Passover celebration to remind themselves that they absolutely needed God because he alone was able to rescue them from slavery.

Third, we use unleavened bread in today's Mass to remind us that, like the escaping Jews, we Christians are a "people on our way," a pilgrim people. We have not quite yet arrived at our heavenly kingdom, thus we need the food of life, Jesus. In addition, we ourselves should be the yeast or leaven which will permeate humanity and help bring it to God the Father.

c. *Wine.* In many cultures, wine is the ordinary drink at meals. It has a festive, joyous quality about it. Wine also has a medicinal function. To make wine, the grapes must undergo the process of fermentation which can be defined as the "rapid growth of a community of minute organisms." Consecrated wine is the Lord's blood. Blood in the scripture is often referred to as the sign of life uniting God with his people. The lamb's blood smeared on the door saved the firstborn son from death. Moses sprinkled blood of the sacrificial victim on the altar and on the people. In the Last Supper Jesus refers to wine as his blood of the New Covenant between God and his people.

We are joyful because we are united to him and his Father and to one another when we drink the consecrated wine. We become a community of love because we are joined to the community of love, the Blessed Trinity. This love also helps cure us of our sinful dispositions and hateful attitudes. It does so because it contains the power of God's love and healing. Jesus alluded to this reality when he said:

"I am the vine, you are the branches.
He who lives in me and I in him,
will produce abundantly,
for apart from me you can do nothing."
(Jn 15:5)

---

**EXERCISE:**

Make a list of other symbols used in the Mass and discuss their significance. For example,

*Candles:* Christ's life and light

*Offertory gifts:* Our concern for all peoples

### Some Symbols of the Eucharist

*Fish and loaves.* Fish (ΙΧΘΥΣ), in Greek lettering, spells out the anagram, "Jesus Christ, Son of God, Savior" and is a traditional symbol for Jesus. The basket of loaves represents the Eucharistic bread and also symbolizes the miracle of the loaves performed by Jesus, which was a sign in his own ministry of the miracle of the Eucharist which was to come.

*Grapes and wheat.* In Christian art, grapes allude to wine which is transformed into our Lord's blood. Shafts of wheat in nativity or adoration scenes foreshadow our Lord's mission of savior of mankind.

Look up other symbols in the *Catholic Encyclopedia.*

---

2. *Eucharist as Celebration.* We often hear the expression "to celebrate the liturgy of the Mass." Just what do we celebrate at Mass? We celebrate many things, but especially we celebrate the Paschal Mystery, that is, the passion, death, resurrection and glorification of Jesus Christ. What this means, in brief, is that Jesus has won salvation for us, he has begun the healing process of reconciliation between God and man and between individuals. We celebrate our Lord's risen presence and his power of love which binds all peoples together. At the Mass, we praise God for accomplishing our salvation and for extending his saving actions here and now in his Son who acts in the lives of people who are saved by him. We praise, worship and thank God for conquering sin and especially death, through the great act of love and obedience of his Son and for extending the fruits of Jesus' love to all of us here and now.

For Discussion:

1. How can we make the Mass more of a *celebration*, a joyful praising of God the Father for the gift of his Son and what he has accomplished for us?

2. How might we practically live out in the Mass the words of Psalm 150?

> Alleluia.
>
> Praise the LORD in his sanctuary,
>     praise him in the firmament of his strength.
> Praise him for his mighty deeds,
>     praise him for his sovereign majesty.
> Praise him with the blast of the trumpet,
>     praise him with lyre and harp,
> Praise him with timbrel and dance,
>     praise him with strings and pipe.
> Praise him with sounding cymbals,
>     praise him with clanging cymbals.
> Let everything that has breath
>     praise the LORD! Alleluia.

3. *Eucharist as Sacrifice.* "Sacrifice" is a word derived from the Latin which means "to make holy or to do something holy." Holiness refers to being one with God, that is, sharing his life, his being, and his love. Only God himself can make us holy, only he can "offer" his holiness to us.

Catholics believe that the Mass is a real sacrifice instituted by our Lord at the Last Supper. It represents the sacrifice of Christ on the Cross, but in an unbloody manner. In the sacrifice Jesus Christ is both the priest and the victim who offers himself through the priest and laity in praise, thanksgiving, petition and atonement.

What is the significance of this sacrifice? In the person of Jesus Christ, both God and man are joined. He is both God and man. Through Christ, God the Father offers us something; Christ is the great sacrament (visible sign or symbol) of God's love. He is God's love. But through the humanity of Jesus, mankind both *receives* and *responds* to the offer of God's love. As man, Jesus was totally open, receptive, obedient and responsive to his Father— even to death. He who was the holy one allowed himself to be treated as though he were not holy by dying on the cross. Unlike the first representative of mankind, Adam, Jesus Christ let himself be put totally in the hands of his Father. By so doing, he sacrificed for us, that is, made us holy, made it possible for us to "be with God," to share his very life.

Today, by offering "the sacrifice of the Mass," we continue to be made holy by accepting the attitude of our brother and Savior Jesus Christ. The result is that the love of God transforms us more and more deeply. By reenacting the sacrifice of Calvary, we are commemorating the death and the resurrection of Jesus. Its profound message is that by dying to self, that is, offering oneself for others, by sacrificing (the crucifixion), superabundant life results (resurrection). Death to self is another term for love. Just as Jesus "broke the bread and gave it to his disciples" and commanded us to "do likewise" in celebrating the sacrifice of the Mass, we should remember to "break ourselves" for others because therein lie love and holiness and true life, the life of Jesus and union with the Father.

*Sacrifice of the Cross.* The great symbol of Christ's act of loving sacrifice is the cross. It is the symbol of a defeated man, of a criminal. Yet, in faith, we see it as a sublime sign of victory, of death's defeat, of love's victory. On the next page are pictured a few Christian crosses with their symbolism explained.

An anchor cross. An anchor is a symbol of hope, thus the Christian's hope rests in our Lord Jesus Christ.

A Celtic cross is sometimes called a "wheel cross" because of the circle (a symbol for God) connecting the beams.

A Christogram. XR (Chi Rho) stands for the first two letters of the word Christ in Greek. In Fig. 4 the X has the form of a cross.

Discuss ways you can "sacrifice":

a. at home
b. at school
c. with your friends

How does each of these show Christ's love?

How is each a "breaking of yourself (bread)"?

4. *Eucharist as Meal.* The Eucharist is a commemorative meal which recalls the Last Supper Jesus celebrated with his apostles. A meal has a festive and intimate quality about it. Around a table gather friends who share the joy of companionship and partake of the same food. The universal symbol of friendship is a shared meal. It signifies a oneness of heart, a unity between friends. In addition, it helps create unity.

An early Christian name for the Eucharist was *agape* which means "love feast." Early Christians were trying to emphasize that when they "broke bread together" they were celebrating the presence of the risen Lord Jesus who called them together and by the power of his life created in them a community of love. Because some lax Christians did not appreciate this meaning of Eucharist, St. Paul was very critical of certain abuses in the celebration of the sacrament at Corinth. Apparently, some Corinthians came to the "love feast" and refused to share their food with the poor who had come or they hurried to get done or they glutted themselves on food or drink (1 Cor 11:17-34). In other words, they did not recognize the presence of the Lord at the Eucharist—they were unaware of Jesus' presence in the breaking of the bread and the sharing of the cup or in their fellow Christians who had come to celebrate with them. Paul admonished very strongly those who were guilty of abuses at Corinth:

> This means that whoever eats the bread or drinks the cup of the Lord unworthily sins against the body and blood of the Lord. A man should examine himself first; only then should he eat of the bread and drink of the cup. He who eats and drinks without recognizing the body eats and drinks a judgment on himself.
>
> (1 Cor 11:27-29)

At the Eucharist, we come to God as we are in all of our weakness, in all of our humanity. We come, moreover, not just to eat, but to savor and enjoy the risen Lord and his life in our fellow Christians. We come actively to share food, the bread of life, Jesus. It is no accident that our Lord presents himself in the form of food to eat and drink to nourish. Food and drink satisfy our basic human need of hunger. Food and drink remind us that without their ultimate source, namely, God the Father, we would die. So, too, without the sharing of our brother Jesus, we would spiritually die.

A meal brings with it warmth and companionship. For the Christian, the Eucharist as a meal is a foretaste of our spiritual inheritance, the heavenly banquet where we will be united totally to God. It is the perfect image of our final destiny of union with our Father and union with our brothers and sisters. Such a union—like any good meal—will bring untold joy and contentment.

To Think About and Discuss:

1. The Eucharist reminds us of our dependence not only on God but also on others. For example, note all the people involved in bringing bread to our table:

    • the person who slices it
    • the one who sells it
    • the one who transports it to the store
    • the one who bakes it
    • the one who grinds it
    • the one who plants it, grows it and harvests it
    • those who supply all the machines to do the above (and all others in the chain of work needed to produce them)
    • the supplier of the seed
    • the mass of other humans who preceded us and who passed on good grain seeds and the knowledge to grow and produce bread

2. In what other ways can you see the Eucharist as a sharing? For example, comment on:

    a. Participation in the songs and prayers by all present

    b. The offertory collection

    c. The dismissal: "Go in peace to love and serve the Lord"

3. Why do you suppose the Church requests that we abstain from food and drink for one hour before we receive the Eucharist?

5. *Eucharist as Ritual.* Rituals play an important part in our lives. Unlike parties, spontaneous or not, rituals have a pattern to them. Note, for example, the ritual of the football rally. A good rally is always well-organized and carefully rehearsed. It builds to a climax which tries to excite the home team crowd into enthusiastic, participative fans who in some way are closely knit to the actual players on the field. Nothing is left to chance.

The liturgy of the Mass is also a ritual. It is a renewal of the new covenant in Jesus Christ. It enables us to enter into the events we celebrate. The ritual of the Eucharist is a patterned remembering of the events Jesus enacted for our salvation. It involves the whole person in symbolic gesturing. For example, the priest

*marches in procession* to indicate that we are *pilgrim* people moving in the present to a glorious future. We stand to show our basic dignity as children of the Father. We kneel to show our reverence and thanksgiving and profess our adoration in humility. We eat and drink from the same table of the Lord, remembering in joy and community who we are and why we are a people and what we are about. We sing, thus stepping out of ordinariness as we celebrate and praise the Lord.

The rite of the Mass consists of two major parts: the liturgy of the Word and the liturgy of the Eucharist. In the liturgy of the Word, we listen to God's word. We derive nourishment from it and are challenged to respond to it.

**LITURGY OF THE WORD.** (We listen and respond to the scriptural word of God.)

1. *Introductory rite*
   procession
   prayer
   song of praise

2. *Liturgy of the Word proper*
   first reading
   Gospel
   homily
   Creed

The liturgy of the Eucharist is the central act of the Mass. Its focal point is the death and resurrection of Jesus; its setting, the Last Supper. Our full participation in the Eucharist culminates in the reception of our Lord under the forms of bread and wine.

**LITURGY OF THE EUCHARIST.** (We join ourselves to Jesus in praise of the Father. We receive the risen Lord as a source of unity, love and strength.)

1. *Liturgy of the Eucharist proper*
   offertory
   Eucharistic prayer
   concluding acclamation

2. *Communion rite*
   Lord's Prayer
   peace sharing
   communion

3. *Concluding rite*
   blessing
   dismissal and the making real of the Mass in life

## WHAT DOES THIS MEAN?

Young people often agree with the theology of the Eucharist but in the last analysis seem most concerned about the Sunday Mass obligation. Their question most often takes this form, "Why should I go to Mass when I don't seem to get anything out of it?" In addition, a common complaint is that so many people who go to Mass seem to be "Sunday Christians," that is, their religion seems to depart the minute they hit the parking lot.

Weekly attendance at Sunday Mass is a fundamental aspect of Catholic life. But to see why this is so we must avoid a mentality which sees attendance at Mass simply as an "obligation." What should prompt a young person and others to attend is not the law of mere physical attendance. The purpose of the law is to remind us of our responsibility to come and join ourselves to our brother Jesus and to one another in worship of the Father. Our attitude should be one of "what can I give to the liturgy," that is, to God and to my fellow Christians who have come to worship. By looking for "what I get out of it," a person is approaching the liturgy from the wrong perspective. To go to Mass, even when it is difficult to do so or when we simply do not feel like going, is to show a great act of love to God and our fellow Christians. We add nothing to the community by our absence; we have everything to give by going.

The second criticism is a valid one. Hypocrites do go to Mass. But the real issue is that we are all hypocrites. We all profess high ideals, but if we are honest with ourselves, we can all admit that we very often fall short of our beliefs. We sin. We are phonies. The point is this: Jesus likes to get involved in the lives of ordinary sinners. He comes to us as we are—weak, fallen, ordinary, often hypocritical. Our religion is not exclusive, for a "goody-goody elite." It is for everyone, including, most especially, sinners. Jesus associated with all kinds during his ministry; the ones he seemed to have least patience for were those who thought they were better than everyone else.

---

To Discuss and To Do:

1. Discuss what the Mass means to you. Why do you go to the Mass? Interview at least three other Catholics for whom you have high regard and ask them these same two questions. Report results to the class.

2. What concrete steps can you as a young person take to make your parish liturgies better? As a class, make a list of things you can do and present them to your pastor(s), volunteering your help.

3. Research the following:

   a. Why do we worship on Sunday, rather than on the Sabbath?

   b. What is the Easter duty and what is the reason for it?

   c. What is the "liturgical year"?

---

## OTHER QUESTIONS

A question many ask about the Mass is: "What is meant by the 'real presence' of Jesus in the Eucharist?" As a matter of fact, one of the distinguishing factors of Catholics is their belief in the "real presence" of the risen Jesus in the elements of bread and wine. We admit of various kinds of presences of Jesus at the Mass. For example, he is present in the reading of his word (the Scripture) and in the preaching of the word. Jesus is also present in the priest who assembles the worshipping community. Furthermore, he is present in the people of God, the congregation of believers. But we admit of a special presence of Jesus in the form of bread and wine. Just exactly how this presence works is a mystery. The Church has used the word *transubstantiation* to express the mystery that at the Consecration of the Mass, the *reality* of the bread and wine, that is, the "breadness" and "wineness" change into the *reality* of Jesus—his risen, glorified body. To receive Jesus in the "species" of the bread or the "species" of the wine is to receive the whole Christ since he is totally present in both species.

The Catholic believes it is a singular privilege to receive our Lord in Holy Communion. In human terms, we cannot be more closely united to Christ (and to one another) than in our reception of the Eucharist.

1. Make a visit on a regular basis to the Blessed Sacrament.

2. What kind of guidelines do you think should be established for behavior in church? Why?

## EVALUATION

Briefly discuss the Eucharist in terms of symbol, celebration, sacrifice, meal, and ritual.

## SUMMARY

The following points help to summarize the main points of the chapter.

1. Liturgy, which is the work of God's people, reaches its fullest expression in the Eucharist which both expresses and creates Christian unity.

2. One can never plumb the depths of the mystery of the Eucharist. However, the following five aspects help us understand it a bit better:

a. *Symbol.* The words read, spoken, and proclaimed at the Mass as well as the bread and the wine are profound symbols of God's presence with us.

b. *Celebration.* In the Eucharist, we celebrate the Paschal Mystery and our union with Christ.

c. *Sacrifice.* The sacrifice of Christ makes us holy and represents in the same act God giving infinite love and man responding to this love.

d. *Meal.* The meal aspect is an agape (love feast) which points to our heavenly banquet with our Father in heaven.

e. *Ritual.* The Mass is a ritual which helps us celebrate and make real in the present who we are and why we are in Christ by remembering the glorious deeds of the past as we move into the future.

3. Mass attendance on Sunday might be more fruitful if we go with an attitude of putting ourselves into it (rather than what one can get out of it) and realizing that Jesus invites us all, sinners and saints, phonies and genuine people, to dine with him.

4. Catholics believe in the real presence of the glorified Jesus Christ in the consecrated bread and wine. Theologians explain the transformation which takes place by the term *transubstantiation* which refers to the mystery in which the reality of the bread and wine changes into the reality of Jesus Christ.

# 10

# The Last Things

*We look for the resurrection of the dead and the life of the world to come.*

(The Nicene Creed)

Most everyone is familiar with the image of the fortune-teller gazing into a crystal ball in an attempt to predict someone's future. The majority of people do not take such efforts seriously. But most right-thinking people do take seriously the matter of their own future destiny as human beings. Human life is often depicted as a kind of journey which begins with birth and ends with death. Seen in this way, the final, universal question of human life is this: "What is our destiny beyond the grave?" Phrased differently, "What does life on earth all add up to? Does death annihilate or fulfill what it means to be a human being?"

*Eschatology* is the name given to the branch of Christian theology which explores the question of ultimate human destiny. The word *eschatology* is derived from the Greek word *eschaton,* meaning "the last thing." In this chapter we will study what is traditionally referred to as the last things of our lives both as human beings and more particularly as disciples of Christ.

**EXERCISES:**

1. In your own words, complete each of the following sentences about life after death as made known to us by our Christian faith.

   Heaven can be described as _____ .

   Hell can be described as _____ .

   The resurrection of the dead refers to _____

   _____ .

   Christ's second coming refers to _____

   _____ .

2. Listed below are a number of different attitudes about death. After each attitude, indicate the kind of person who might hold such an attitude. Then indicate a Christian response to each.

| BASIC ATTITUDE | KIND OF PERSON | CHRISTIAN RESPONSE |
|---|---|---|
| Death is depressing. We should put death out of our minds and cram as much pleasure into our lives as we can. | | |
| Because of the universal reality of death, life itself is depressing. "The heartbeat is but a muffled funeral march to the grave." | | |
| Because of death we must make each day count, living each day as though it were our last. | | |
| We should love life and face death in the hope of sharing in Christ's resurrection. | | |

In this chapter we will discuss the topic of eschatology under the three main headings of:

1. The New Testament teaching on eternal life
2. The ongoing tradition of the believing community's faith in life after death
3. Christian attitudes toward death
4. Mary — Model of the new creation

## NEW TESTAMENT ESCHATOLOGY

As presented in the New Testament, eschatology has both *present* and *future* aspects. The "last thing" is already present within us in that Christ has already restored us to union with the Father. Thus, our daily, baptized, faith-filled Christian life is, in fact, an eternal life for Christ. Our Life will never leave us to face our perils alone.

This notion of eschatology is expressed most frequently in the writings of St. John. At the conclusion to his first letter he writes, "I have written this to you to make you realize that you possess eternal life—you who believe in the name of the Son of God." A few lines previous to this St. John specifies:

> The testimony is this:
> God gave us eternal life,
> and this life is in his Son.
> Whoever possesses the Son
> possesses life.
>
> (1 Jn 5:11-12)

The eternal life Jesus came to give us is sometimes referred to by Jesus in terms of the Kingdom of God. Jesus tells us that in him the Kingdom has already been established and that all who believe in him should rejoice for they are members of his Father's kingdom.

*The Already and the Not Yet*

In order to appreciate the future aspect of Christian eschatology imagine for a moment an engaged couple who are very much in love. In one sense, they *already* have each other. The love they share is truly present to both. Yet there is a strong, future-oriented aspect to their relationship. Both long for the day when they can be truly one as husband and wife. Somehow their period of engagement is a time when they are not yet fully together to the extent their love for each other demands.

A similar situation exists for the Christian here on earth. We are now truly with Christ in faith. He is in our hearts through the indwelling of the Spirit. He nourishes us with himself in the Eucharist and he gives us the strength to try to be kind, generous, sincere, that is, Christlike in our daily dealings with others. We are even now children of God, members of the Father's kingdom. But at the same time we are *not yet* able to *know* and *experience* fully the eternal life which is ours through Christ. There is the matter of our own physical illness and eventual death. There are our ever-present weaknesses and failings. There are numerous occasions when we seem to be struggling against unbearable odds. Thus, we are truly with Christ and, at the same time, we are not yet fully united with him in such a way as to free us from weakness, hardship and death.

Just as the engaged couple longs for some future union so, too, we Christians on earth long for some future, more perfect union with Christ. Christ promised that this longed-for union between him and his disciples would occur at his second coming in glory at the end of time. Then, he promised that the Kingdom of God now present (yet hidden) will become fully manifested on that day when he comes to judge the living and the dead and to establish forever his Father's kingdom. What follows is a brief synthesis of the New Testament teachings about the *eschaton,* that is, the final coming of Christ at the end of time.

*The Signs.* Jesus said that his coming will be preceded by definite warnings or signs. The Gospel of Luke reports that Jesus spoke of these signs saying,

> "There will be signs in the sun, the moon and the stars. On the earth, nations will be in anguish, distraught at the roaring of the sea and the waves. Men will die of fright in anticipation of what is coming upon the earth. The powers in the heavens will be shaken. After that men will see the Son of Man coming on a cloud with power and glory.
> When these things begin to happen, stand erect and hold your heads high, for your deliverance is near at hand."
>
> (Lk 21:25-28)

It is interesting to note that some texts do not speak of such warnings but stress the point that Jesus will come without warning like a thief in the night at an hour when we least expect, or like lightning flashing without warning from the east to the west.

*The Resurrection of the Dead.* Those who have died will be reunited with their resurrected bodies. The bodies of the blessed will reflect their share in the resurrected life of Christ. The bodies of the damned will bear the marks of disfigurement and sin.

*Christ's Second Coming.* With time at an end and the dead risen from their graves, Christ will return to earth in glory and majesty. All of humanity will see that he is truly the *Kyrios,* the Lord.

*The Judgment.* Jesus the Lord will then judge the human family. In the imagery Jesus himself uses:

> "When the son of Man comes in his glory, escorted by all the angels of heaven, he will sit upon his royal throne, and all the nations will be assembled before him. Then he will separate them into two groups, as a shepherd separates sheep from goats. The sheep he will place on his right hand, the goats on his left. The King will say to those on his right: 'Come. You have my Father's blessing!

Inherit the kingdom prepared for you from the creation of the world.' . . .
"Then he will say to those on his left: 'Out of
my sight, you condemned, into that everlasting fire
prepared for the devil and his angels!' "
(Mt 25:31-41)

*The Establishing of the Kingdom.* Finally, Christ will establish
his Father's kingdom, a perfect social unity of justice and love. In
a heaven of perfect happiness and on an earth recreated in Christ,
all the blessed will forever enjoy a communal life free of prejudice,
hatred, injustice, suffering and death.

*New Heaven and a New Earth.* The second coming of Christ and
the establishing of the Father's kingdom will not mark the end of
God's creation. On the contrary, the universe is destined to share
in the glory of the resurrected Jesus who will establish a new heaven
and a new earth. St. Paul speaks as though the universe is in birth
pains giving birth to its own future perfection in Christ. The
beauties of the universe and especially our physical bodies are destined by God to share in the eternal glory of the Father's kingdom.

---

For Discussion:

1. What if you discovered that tomorrow will be the day
   of Christ's second coming, that tomorrow life on this
   earth as you know it will end and that Christ will judge
   you and all humanity? Write a paragraph or two describing what changes this would have on the way you
   lived the rest of today. What would you do today that
   you have been putting off? What "important things"
   would suddenly seem unimportant and what seemingly
   unimportant things would appear to be very important?
   When finished, share your ideas with the students in
   your class.

2. As a class read Revelations 20-23 and 1 Cor 15. Share
   together what these two texts tell us about the eschaton.

---

The New Testament eschatology describes Christ's second
coming at the end of time when he will judge the living and the
dead and establish forever his Father's Kingdom. In general, the
writers of the New Testament felt convinced that this second com-

ing was going to happen in the very near future. In light of this conviction, the New Testament offers us few texts that explicitly refer to the "interim state," that is, that state of the dead between biological death and the second coming.

Our Catholic tradition, however, developed over the centuries the realization that Christ's second coming was going to be delayed much longer than the New Testament writers imagined. This reflection in the Church's tradition, guided by the Holy Spirit, offers us a rich heritage of belief about the nature of life after death before the second coming of Christ. It is the content of this tradition which we will discuss here.

## BELIEF IN LIFE AFTER DEATH AS EXPRESSED IN THE TRADITION OF THE CHURCH

### The Particular Judgment

The term "particular judgment" refers to the Christian belief that God judges each person individually immediately after death. There is no text in scripture which states outright that there is a particular judgment. However, several texts do imply that there is such a judgment, as does, for example, the story of Lazarus and the rich man (Lk 13:24-28). Belief in the particular judgment developed gradually in the tradition of the Church. By the year 1274 at the Council of Lyons, the Church stated the belief that the reward of heaven or the punishment of hell begins *immediately* after death. Such a position necessitates some kind of judgment by God immediately after death.

Several important points regarding the particular judgment are: first, no actual vision of God occurs in the judgment. The vision of God is the essential reward of the blessed in heaven. Secondly, in the particular judgment, God is not like a judge sitting before us holding a huge book open to a list of all our thoughts and actions while on earth. In a sense, our life on earth is our judge. All our days either add up to a sincere desire to be one with God in Christ or they add up to a free, final decision to reject God and separate ourselves from him forever. The particular judgment draws our attention to the sovereign power God has over us. It is God who judges us. His judgment is without error. It is loving and just. It is the *truth* of whether or not we accepted or rejected him while on earth.

Thirdly, the Good News of the gospel is that in a sense we are already judged and that God has judged us with forgiveness. It is our task to accept this forgiveness which comes to us in Christ. The gospel of St. John especially stresses this point: judgment is already at work for God is even now judging us according to whether or not we accept Christ as our Savior.

---

For Discussion:

1. Understanding the word "fear" to mean awe or reverence, discuss how the particular judgment helps us to understand the Old Testament statement that, "Fear of the Lord is the beginning of wisdom."

2. Do you think it is important that we are held accountable for our lives? Why should the idea of the particular judgment help us always to be honest with ourselves?

---

*Heaven*

Those judged by God to be saved enter into the everlasting reward of eternal life in heaven. The essence of heaven is the vision of God (traditionally called the "beatific vision" because it is the vision that brings perfect beatitude, that is, happiness). God created us with the intention that we live on earth in such a way so as to enter into an eternal sharing of his own divine life. Thus, heaven is our one, final, perfect human fulfillment for it is in God alone that we as persons will be made perfectly happy.

Along with the vision of God, the blessed also enjoy their union with one another. All the blessed form a community of perfect unity and love that make up the Kingdom of God. In heaven there are not the misunderstanding and struggle that often accompany human relationships on earth. God created us as social beings. He called us to salvation in the community of the Church and in heaven we will enjoy our life-giving union with God in the company of all the angels and saints.

---

Discuss:

When we come to see God "face to face" what do you think will surprise us the most about God? What do you think we will see in God that will move us the most to love him? What do you think we will see in God that will make us the happiest?

What moments of life on earth do you think come the closest to resembling the happiness of heaven? After listing and discussing these moments, discuss what love has to do with each of the human experiences discussed.

---

*Hell*

Jesus taught that his heavenly Father is all-loving and merciful. But he also taught that his Father is all-just. God created us with a free will and he accepts our free decision to have faith in him and follow his will or to reject him and live a life of sin. The eternal consequence of freely choosing to seek God is called heaven. The eternal consequence of freely choosing a life of sin is called hell.

Jesus spoke often of hell as a state of everlasting separation from God. He also spoke of it in terms of a place of suffering resulting from that separation (Lk 16:22, Mk 9:43, cf Mt 25:31).

The essence of heaven is union with God and the essence of hell is separation from God. The pain of hell is the pain of having been created for union with God and yet, through one's own free choice, being deprived of that union for all eternity. Along with this pain of separation, scripture and the tradition of the Church also teach there is a pain resulting from the selfish use of created pleasures during one's life on earth. Traditionally, this pain is expressed in the imagery of fire, but actually we do not know precisely what the nature of this pain is.

---

*To Think About:*

What does Jesus' teaching about the existence of hell tell us about the seriousness of our life on earth? What does it tell us about the fact that once God creates us as persons with a free will he never violates our free decision to reject him by a life of sin?

---

*Purgatory*

Many Christians die in a state of being sincere and genuine in their efforts to be a follower of Christ. Yet, they die under the influence of venial sin or before they are able, by way of prayer and Christlike service to others, to do penance for their past sins. The Church teaches that such people must first be purified before entering heaven. This state of purifying, or purging, is called purgatory. Those in purgatory are happy in that they know beyond doubt that they are destined for heaven. But they are saddened as well by their temporary separation from God. This separation causes them a kind of pain which the tradition of the Church has likened to the pain caused by fire. The Church also teaches that the prayers of those on earth can hasten the deliverance of the "poor souls" from the pains of purgatory into the happiness of heaven.

Belief in purgatory is based not only on the long Spirit-guided tradition of the Church, but also in an important text of scripture found in the second book of Maccabees. In this text, a man named Judas offers gifts for those who have died. Commenting on his action, the text reads,

> "But if he did this with a view to the splendid reward
> that awaits those who have gone to rest in godliness,
> it was a holy and pious thought. Thus he made
> atonement for the dead that they might be freed
> from this sin" (2 Mac 12:45).

In the past, the tradition of the Church has considered purgatory to be a kind of place in which the souls in purgatory stay for a certain duration of time. Today in the ongoing tradition of the Church, some Catholic theologians are speaking of purgatory as the instantaneous experience of meeting the risen Jesus. In Christ's loving gaze our own past infidelity "burns" us to the degree which we failed to respond to his love. As we are "burned" by the fire of his love we are also purified of the effects of sin and are thus able to enter into the kingdom of heaven.

---

For Discussion:

1. In the past, certain patristic writings of the Church held that many people go to hell and few people enter heaven. Today, most theologians would tend to say that most people are in heaven because being damned calls for a free, deliberate, total rejection of God which is rarely found. Have a discussion to determine what the class feels about the question of hell and how many people go there. Comment on the fact that the Church has never stated that anyone, even Judas, is in hell.

2. November 2 is All Souls' Day and the whole month of November is set aside to remember in a special way those in purgatory. What are your feelings toward loved ones who have died? Do you think they can see and hear us? That they still love us? Do you think they are still close to us? Do our prayers for them allow us to continue a kind of hidden relationship that will be made fully known to us in the hour of our own deaths?

---

### Christian Attitudes Toward Death

The following three exercises are intended to help you apply the notions of life and death (as understood by a Christian) to your daily life.

1. Reflection on eternity as a never-ending conscious relationship with God can help us see our life on earth in a new perspective. As a class, reflect on the following idea: Without the idea of eternity, a long life on earth seems long indeed. But in contrast to eternity, even the longest of human lives is but a fleeting moment. This idea is illustrated in the line below. The line represents eternity. The arrow to the right indicates that eternity never ends. The short vertical line at the left indicates birth and the X stands for death at the end of a "long life."

2. In the exercise below indicate how each activity mentioned necessitates a kind of death to self (a carrying of our cross) on our part. Then indicate how each activity can also provide an occasion for us to experience our eternal life with Christ by making us aware of a deeper level of love between ourselves, God and others.

Taking part in a school program to collect and deliver canned food to the poor

A death to self _____

A taste of eternal life
_____

Making an effort to communicate with your parents

A death to self _____
_____

A taste of eternal life
_____

Going to Sunday Mass, receiving Communion in a mature and sincere effort to draw closer to Christ

A death to self _____

A taste of eternal life
_____

Going out of your way to make friends with a new student who is ignored or even made fun of by others

A death to self _____
_____

A taste of eternal life
_____

3. Jesus' glorified body still bears the marks of his crucifixion. His resurrected glory is the eternal unfolding of his life and death on earth. Jesus has told us that the same is true of us. Our life on earth, though short, is of eternal value. In the kingdom of God our daily deaths to self and our daily tastes of eternal life will bear an eternal harvest of life with Christ in the kingdom of God.

Go back to the exercise #2 above. Consider the answers you gave on the spaces marked "a taste of eternal life" to be instead "hints of eternal life." Use your answers as a basis for writing a paragraph titled "What the kingdom of God is like." After sharing your ideas as a class discuss the eternal value of such things as prison reform, world hunger relief programs, the rights of the mentally handicapped, etc. In light of your discussion what does it mean to "prepare for God's kingdom"?

## MARY—MODEL OF THE NEW CREATION

On November 1, 1950, Pope Pius XII formally defined the Dogma of the Assumption of Mary bodily into heaven by decreeing, "We proclaim, declare and define it to be a dogma revealed by God that the immaculate mother of God, Mary ever virgin, when the course of her earthly life was finished, was taken up body and soul into the glory of heaven."

Though recent in formal declaration, belief in the bodily assumption has an ancient and sacred tradition in the Church. As early as around the year 500, the Eastern Church celebrated the feast of the Dormition of Mary, her "falling asleep" in the Lord. By about the middle of the eighth century, St. John Damascene expressed a fully developed belief in the bodily assumption of Mary.

The unique privilege of Mary being assumed bodily into heaven stems from her unique privilege of being the mother of God conceived free of original sin. In her assumption, she is preserved from the decay of death. Furthermore, our Christian hope lies in the prospect of sharing in the resurrection of Jesus. Mary the mother of Jesus is the first to share in his resurrection. In doing so she becomes a living model of the Church in its future destiny of unity with the risen Christ. Mary is, in other words, a living model of Christian eschatology. She is a model of the new human-ity born of her son, the new Adam, who brought eternal life to all who believe in him. As the Second Vatican Council's *Constitution on the Church* expressed it,

> In the bodily and spiritual glory which she possesses in heaven, the mother of Jesus continues in this pres-ent world as the image and first flowering of the Church as she is to be perfected in the world to come.
>
> (*Lumen Gentium*, 68)

**EXERCISES:**

1. Some students in the class can look up the readings for the feast of the Assumption. The class can discuss the readings in the light of Christian eschatology as out-lined in this chapter.

2. The class can say the glorious mysteries of the rosary together as a form of class prayer. How do these mysteries help make us aware of the main elements of Christian eschatology? What is Mary's place in the whole picture of Christian eschatology?

3. A group in the class can look up the readings for the feast of the Immaculate Conception. What light do these readings throw on the place of Mary in God's plan of salvation?

## WHAT DOES THIS MEAN?

All human life ends in death. If there is no life beyond death it means that the eternal life promised to us by Christ is not eternal at all. At best, Christianity offers us but a passing source of con-solation and moral guidance during our brief span on earth. It would also mean that all our efforts as Christians to live as Christ did, to feed the poor and help the oppressed, are of no lasting sig-nificance. It would mean, in fact, that Christ's own death on the cross was futile. It would mean he failed in his mission to grant us a share in the eternal life he shares with his Father. In short, Chris-tian life would make no sense whatsoever without life after death. But because of the reality of life after death as promised to us by

Christ, our life on earth is given a meaning of eternal significance. It means we can face all our troubles and even our death with a sense of hope and confidence in God. We can turn to our joys and triumphs knowing that in Christ nothing of value in our life will ever be lost. Everything in our life that is true and beautiful, everything that is of love is forever.

## OTHER QUESTIONS

### Do Unbaptized Babies Go to Heaven?

As we saw in the chapter on the sacraments, the Church teaches that no one can enter heaven without first in some way being baptized in Christ. We saw too that baptism must be conferred either by water (the rite of baptism), by blood (the martyrs), or by desire (those who have never been given the gift of faith but who die with a good conscience indicating that they would have accepted Christ had they been given the opportunity to know him).

This realization of the necessity of baptism raises a problem concerning the eternal salvation of those who are unbaptized and who die in infancy. Of course, the unbaptized babies cannot go to hell or purgatory since they have done nothing wrong. Yet, they have not had the opportunity to have baptism by desire since they have not yet had any opportunity to love others or to choose good over evil. St. Thomas Aquinas and others concluded that these babies go to *Limbo* which is an eternal state of perfect natural happiness without the vision of God.

Revelation does not actually tell us the answer to this question. Nor has the Church ever made any formal, doctrinal statement about it. Today, however, most Catholic theologians would probably be inclined to say that somehow unbaptized babies do enter into the vision of God, that is, into heaven. If not, they conclude, the victory of Satan over Adam and Eve is greater than the victory of Christ on the cross who opened for us the gates of heaven. At any rate, the Church, respecting the fact that we simply do not know the answer to this question, still urges Catholic parents to have their children baptized without unnecessary delay.

For Discussion:

As a class discuss the question of the eternal salvation of babies who die before being baptized.

## SUMMARY

1. In one sense, the kingdom of God has already been established by Christ. We live in the kingdom by our daily life of faith in Christ and our daily death to self in Christ-like love and service to others.

2. Our daily life of faith has eternal value, for Christ is to come at the end of the world to judge all humanity and to establish his Father's kingdom as a kingdom of eternal, universal justice and love.

3. In the tradition of the Church, heaven, hell and purgatory are the three states of existence that are possible for us after death. Heaven is essentially an eternal face-to-face vision of God in the community of all the angels and saints. Hell is essentially an eternal separation from God and the pain resulting from that separation. Purgatory is a state of purification prior to entering heaven.

4. The Assumption of Mary provides us with a living symbol of the New Humanity in union with the risen Christ.

## EVALUATION

In light of all you have learned in this chapter, go back and look at the answers you gave in the opening exercise of this chapter. What changes or additions would you possibly wish to make in your answers?

## ADDITIONAL EXERCISES:

1. Have a group in the class bring in a copy of the present funeral Mass as well as a copy of the funeral Mass used before the Second Vatican Council. As a group, discuss the differences in tone and emphasis in these two liturgies.

2. Some in the class can agree to read either *Spoon River Anthology* by Edgar Lee Masters, *Green Pastures* by Marc Connelly, or *Our Town* by Thornton Wilder. What imagery and themes do these well-known plays use to develop their concepts of life after death? How do these concepts compare/contrast with that of Christian tradition?

3. Some in the class may enjoy looking at Dante's *The Divine Comedy*. A short essay can be written on one's impressions of reading bits and pieces of this classic work about hell, purgatory and heaven.

4. The Hymn "Dies Irae" can be found in the old Roman Missal. It can be read aloud in class and all can reflect on their impressions of its imagery and tone.

5. The book *Life After Life* by Raymond A. Moody, Jr., and the work of Elizabeth Kuebler-Ross, both record many instances of people who have clinically "died" and returned to tell their experiences. A group in the class can research the findings of Doctors Moody and Ross and make a report to the class.

6. A group in the class can interview a Jehovah's Witness concerning their beliefs about the kingdom of God and the end of the world.

# 11

# Catholic Identity and Contemporary Catholic Concerns

*"You are the salt of the earth. But what if salt goes flat?*
*How can you restore its flavor? Then it is good for nothing*
*but to be thrown out and trampled underfoot.*

*"You are the light of the world. A city set on a hill cannot*
*be hidden. Men do not light a lamp and then put it under*
*a bushel basket. They set it on a stand where it gives light*
*to all in the house. In the same way, your light must shine*
*before men so that they may see goodness in your acts and*
*give praise to your heavenly Father."*

(Mt 5:13-16)

We live in a time when people are ever more concerned about their roots. People like to know where their ancestors came from, what they did for a living, how they lived their lives and when they died. Many pay vast sums of money to trace their family tree and usually take great pride in what they find out. Our families give us a sense of identity, a sense of who we are, a feeling of belonging to something bigger than ourselves. This feeling of belonging gives us a community we can call our own. Rightly so, our roots bring us security and pride.

The question is: do we derive the same kind of pride and security from belonging to our family of faith known as the Roman Catholic Church? Unfortunately, perhaps for too many people, our Catholic religion is taken for granted and often is not appreciated. There are many who do not mind being called "Christian" but balk at being termed "Catholic." Why is this so? Maybe it is because many of the traditional symbols of Catholicism no longer apply. It used to be easy to identify Catholics—they did not eat meat on Friday, they fasted during Lent, their Mass was in Latin, their religious sisters all wore identifiable habits. But these factors really are quite superficial. In reality, a Catholic belongs to a community of believers who share Jesus' vision and respond to his presence in their midst. They belong within the context of a particular structure—a structure which helps keep alive and growing the community's spirituality and mission. Suffice it to say here, the major distinguishing factor of a Catholic Christian and other Christian religions is his or her belief that Jesus established a *hierarchical* church (with the pope as vicar of Christ) with a *sacramental spirituality* which celebrates in a unique way the real presence of Christ especially in the Eucharist. The Catholic also believes the Church's never-ending mission is to preach the gospel to all people and be a real sign of Christ serving them.

This chapter will deal with three issues, all of which concern us as Catholics today. The first issue will be the strong stand we in our community take on respect for life. For example, we can be proud of our communal stand on abortion and euthanasia. The second topic will be a brief discussion of the real possibility of finding Jesus within the Church. Unfortunately, too often some young people go searching for Jesus in cults and strange religions and neglect their own privileged position of contacting the Lord Jesus within the Catholic Church. Finally, we will briefly allude to the relationship of other religions to the Catholic Church and discuss what our attitude should be to members of other religions.

Before we take up our first topic, namely respect for life, please do the following exercise and discuss it with your fellow classmates.

**EXERCISE:**

1. What is the first word that comes to mind when you see the word:

   a. Christian _____

   b. Catholic _____

   Are these negative or positive reactions? Explain.

2. What does it mean for you to be a *Catholic* Christian?

3. If you identify yourself as a Catholic, why do you do so?

4. Interview at least two people you admire who are practicing Catholics and ask them the first three questions above. Share their answers with your classmates.

5. If it were a crime to be a Catholic Christian, would there be enough evidence to convict you? Explain.

6. Our definition of a Catholic included several elements: a *community of believers,* with the *vision of Jesus,* in the context of a *church structure* which keeps alive a certain *spirituality* and a *mission.* In small groups, make five short statements which get at the essence of each of these dimensions. Share and discuss these with the other groups.

   a. Community of Believers: (e.g., all members are equal)

      (1) _____

      (2) _____

      (3) _____

      (4) _____

      (5) _____

   b. Vision of Jesus: (e.g., "love one's enemies")

      (1) _____

      (2) _____

      (3) _____

(4) _____

(5) _____

  c.  Church Structure: (e.g., pope—vicar of Christ)

    (1) _____

    (2) _____

    (3) _____

    (4) _____

    (5) _____

  d. Spirituality: (e.g., centrality of the Eucharist)

    (1) _____

    (2) _____

    (3) _____

    (4) _____

    (5) _____

  e. Mission: (e.g., preach gospel)

    (1) _____

    (2) _____

    (3) _____

    (4) _____

    (5) _____

## CATHOLICS STAND FOR LIFE

*Abortion.* It has become clear in recent years that the Catholic community has taken a strong pro-life stand, especially in America. Ever since the landmark Supreme Court decisions in 1973 establishing the civil legality of abortion, the Church has taken a leading role in trying to sensitize the consciences of men and women to the rights of the unborn. As a result of the strong stand on life issues, Catholics and others who support the pro-life movement have often had to pay the cost of their position by receiving strong criticism and even ridicule by many in the media and those advocating abortion on demand. These critics argue that a minority religious group has no right to force others to adopt its moral positions.

The basic difference between pro-lifers and those permitting abortion resides in whether abortion is a medical or moral issue. In its abortion opinions, the Supreme Court asserted that the abortion decision "is inherently and primarily a medical decision, and basic responsibility for it must rest with the physician." The Church does not deny that abortion represents a medical question, but the Church holds that abortion itself is fundamentally a moral question. Genetics, biology and fetology have accumulated enough evidence to demonstrate that each individual human life begins at fertilization, that is, when the female egg and male sperm unite to form a new genetically distinct, human life. *Because we are dealing with a human life, the life of the unborn baby is of value to us.* It is of value because human life is a great gift of God. *Its presence is the basis of the dignity of the human person and all human rights.* In the words of Vatican II:

> All should be persuaded that human life and the task of transmitting it are not realities bound up with this world alone. Hence they cannot be measured or perceived only in terms of it, but always have a bearing on the eternal destiny of men. . . . For God, the Lord of life, has conferred on men the surpassing ministry of safeguarding life in a manner which is worthy of man. Therefore from the moment of its conception life must be guarded with the greatest care, while abortion and infanticide are unspeakable crimes. (*Constitution on the Church in the Modern World*)

To Discuss and Research:

1. Consider the following facts about a fetus:

   - *At conception:* genetically, mother and baby are separate individuals

   - *25 days:* heart starts beating

   - *30 days:* human brain formed as well as eyes, ears, mouth, kidneys, liver and umbilical cord

   - *45 days:* skeleton complete in cartilage, not bone; milk teeth buds appear; baby moves

   - *63 days:* baby can grasp an object placed in its hand and make a fist

   The question is: Should we value this human life and protect and safeguard it? The Church's constant teaching is that we should because we are dealing with a human being who has been granted the gift of life by the Creator.

2. What kinds of reasons do people give for getting abortions? List several. With your teacher, try to find an explanation why each of these reasons, in the last analysis, is unacceptable.

3. *Consider:* There are more abortions in the city of New York than there are live births.

4. Catholics are often accused of imposing their morality on others by supporting pro-life issues. Is this a legitimate criticism in a democracy which allows for minority dissent? Furthermore, where innocent, helpless human life is concerned, must not someone come to their defense, even if others do not agree that month-old or six-month-old fetuses are human?

5. A friend comes to you and says she has gotten pregnant and will soon get an abortion. What would you say to her and why?

6. Write a letter to some political figure or newspaper expressing your beliefs on the right-to-life issues.

*Euthanasia.* Euthanasia means "easy death." It most often refers to actions taken to hasten painlessly the death of someone, thus the term "mercy killing." Usually, the advocates of euthanasia intend to help those suffering from tragic diseases and accidents but all too often its potential application is suggested for helpless invalids, bedridden cripples and the unproductive aged.

The Church fosters respect for human life no matter how young or old, how strong or weak, regardless of one's physical, mental or emotional condition. Human life is sacred of itself apart from its ability to serve as a means of productivity. A person is sacred not only because he or she is a person, but because he or she is made to God's image and likeness, saved by our Lord Jesus Christ, and destined for union with the Father in eternity.

The Catholic Church is in the forefront in condemning all direct and intentional acts which have as their purpose the taking of human life as in the case of active euthanasia. "Whatever is opposed to life itself, such as any type of murder, genocide, abortion, euthanasia, and willful self-destruction . . . all these things and others of their like are infamies indeed. They poison human society, but they do more harm to those who do them than to those who suffer the injury. Moreover, they are a supreme dishonor to the Creator" (*Pastoral Constitution on the Church in the Modern World*).

Christians "affirm life" and manifest this when they do all they can to fight against whatever threatens life—hunger, disease, floods and other natural disasters. However, Christians do not deny the reality of death. We are creatures, thus we are mortal. We have to die in order to be fully united with the Lord. Hence, keeping a person alive regardless of the cost is not an absolute value. On the contrary, Church teaching holds that we must use ordinary means to prolong life (and thus manifest respect for life) but we are not obligated to use extraordinary means to keep a person alive. A terminally ill patient does have a right to die—the use of extraordinary means involving complicated medical procedures or grave expenses to the family need not be employed to prolong a life destined for union with the Creator. Here we are clearly stating that mercy killing (euthanasia) is not the same thing as the refusal to take extraordinary measures to prolong life.

*Two final words:* 1. Proponents of euthanasia ignore the Christian concept of suffering which maintains that suffering is not purely negative. For a Christian, suffering can purify and make holy if the one suffering accepts it in a spirit of penance and is resigned to the will of God.

2. Admittedly, euthanasia presents many challenging moral questions that have no easy answers. For example, not only our ability to maintain life almost indefinitely in some cases, but also the fact that what is an "extraordinary means" today will be an "ordinary means" tomorrow can both raise morally complex questions. But the one guiding principle at work in all these problems is the sacredness of human life which forbids us from actively performing any action which causes death.

## JESUS, THE CATHOLIC CHURCH AND OTHER RELIGIONS

It sometimes happens that young people are attracted for some reason or another to religions other than Christianity and the Catholic faith. "Jesus people" cults and Eastern religions have had special appeal to American youth in recent times. It is difficult to generalize about the "Jesus people" because they represent so many different groups, but their appeal has apparently been their simplified approach to the gospel and their communal life-style. On the other hand, the Eastern religions put a major stress on various forms of contemplative and meditative prayer. Perhaps, though, many who have left the Church in search for the values extolled by these religions have failed to appreciate their own Catholic tradition.

As discussed in the chapter on prayer, the Roman Catholic Church has a rich tradition of prayer in its history, which in recent years is being rediscovered and appreciated anew. Similarly, the Church has a rich variety of life-styles to accommodate many individual responses to the gospel demands. For example, many religious communities of men and women engaged in various apostolates serve the Church. Likewise, there exist institutes of laymen and women who live a life of prayer and service while engaged in the workaday world. Retreat programs like Teens Encounter Christ are available to help young people learn to pray and become closer to Christ. There are even programs (for example, the Jesuit Volunteer Corps) modelled on the Peace Corps, through which youth can devote a year or two of their lives in service to their fellow humans.

To Do:

1. Invite representatives from various religious communities to class to discuss their Christian life-styles and their unique spiritualities.

2. Go to the pastor of your parish to learn about the activities available for young people in the parish. Volunteer your help and involvement in the parish.

## THE CATHOLIC ATTITUDE TOWARD OTHER RELIGIONS

A raging debate among some people in past centuries has been which religion is the one, true religion. The debate was kindled by the Protestant Reformation when various Christian denominations appeared and tried to identify themselves as the true Christian community Jesus founded. The debate took the form of accentuating the differences between the Catholic Church and the various Protestant denominations and downplaying any similarities or common beliefs held by Christian groups. Unfortunately, this gave way to a great deal of misunderstanding and sometimes caused acts of unkindness between Catholic and non-Catholic Christians.

Today, we live in an ecumenical age. "Ecumenism" comes from a Greek word meaning "universal" and refers to a movement among world religions to gain a better understanding of one another and to overcome any needless antagonism. Christians involved in the movement are trying to set up better relationships with the Jews and other world religions and to strive for better unity among themselves.

In its teaching, however, the Catholic Church has not denied that the fullness of Christ's grace and truth is found in itself. We firmly believe and teach that the Church Jesus Christ intended to establish subsists (that is, is to be found) in the Roman Catholic Church. However, the Catholic Church now openly teaches that the Holy Spirit works in all people of good will, in order to build up God's kingdom. It teaches as well that Protestant Christians (though not fully united with the seat of Rome as begun by Peter) are truly members of the Church by virtue of their faith in Christ and their baptism.

Every Catholic can help foster Christian unity. This is done by:

1. *Prayer.* The Holy Spirit is ultimately the source of all unity. Jesus himself promised, "The Father will give you anything you ask him in my name" (Jn 15:16). This is the most important element in the ecumenical movement. It means not only praying for the unity of all Christians but also praying *with* non-Catholic Christians.

2. *Study.* The more one knows one's own traditions, the better he or she will be able to share the truths of the Catholic faith with others. How we state our truths (doctrine) and what we mean by them are important things to know, if we are going to help others to understand. Likewise, people from other faiths will appreciate our having more than just a passing knowledge of their religion.

3. *Communication.* True dialogue and honest and open exchange plus a genuine respect for the views of others help communication. Communication, by definition, means sharing, that is, coming into union.

4. *Cooperation.* Working together on projects of social action fosters the kind of "shoulder rubbing" which demonstrates true witness to gospel values. The experience of serving one's fellow humans goes a long way in bringing people together.

## CATHOLICS AND OTHER CHRISTIAN RELIGIONS

*The Eastern Orthodox.* The Eastern Orthodox Church merits a unique respect from the Catholic Church. Though there are some differences in belief, the Eastern Orthodox churches keep all the basic beliefs and traditions of the Roman Catholic Church up to their separation in 1084. They celebrate all the sacraments and have a valid hierarchy and priesthood. They differ with us over the role of the pope who they claim does not have jurisdiction over the whole Church.

*Protestants.*  The different Protestant churches vary widely in their Christian beliefs and practices.  The four basic Protestant groups are: 1. Anglicans (Episcopalians), 2. Calvinistic (Presbyterians), 3. Lutherans, and 4. other groups.  They "are accepted as brothers by the children of the Catholic Church" (*Decree on Ecumenism,* 3) and have much to offer Catholics, for example, devotion to the Scriptures.  The Catholic Church, too, has much to offer the Protestant denominations, not the least of which is our long tradition which dates back to the apostles.

## CATHOLICS AND NON-CHRISTIAN RELIGIONS

*Jewish Faith.*  We owe the Jewish faith special reverence and respect.  Christianity finds its roots in Judaism.  Jesus was a pious Jew who loved his religion.  Jews have not ceased to be God's chosen people.  They witness to the Father of Jesus and revere the books of the Old Testament which Christians so greatly honor.  Furthermore, they live by the same moral code handed down to Moses (the Ten Commandments).

Unfortunately, much of the history of Christian-Jewish relations has been sad and regrettable.  Anti-Semitism (prejudice directed toward Jews) is against our Lord's call to love.

*Moslems.*  Moslems hold the faith of Abraham and "along with us adore the one and merciful God, who on the last day will judge mankind" (*Lumen Gentium,* 16).  They do not acknowledge the divinity of Jesus but revere him as a great prophet and they honor his mother.  Though in past centuries Christians and Moslems have been at loggerheads, the Vatican II document entitled the "Declaration of the Church to Non-Christian Religions" states that all should "forget the past and strive for mutual understanding, and, on behalf of all mankind, make common cause of safeguarding and fostering social justice, moral values, peace, and freedom" (3).

*Hinduism, Buddhism and Others.*  The Church affirms whatever is holy and good in non-Christian religions.  We respect those ways of conduct and life which reflect God's truth which enlightens all peoples. We recognize that in his own mysterious way God extends his saving love to them. For "the divine design of salvation embraces all men; and those who without fault on their part do not know the Gospel of Christ and his Church, but seek God sincerely, and under the influence of grace endeavor to do his will as recognized through the promptings of conscience, they, in a number known only to God, can attain salvation" (Pope Paul VI, "The Credo of the People of God").

Even those with no professed faith deserve our respect as persons. Those who are open to God's activity in their lives (even if they do not know him) are responding to his salvation. Love is the measure of response to God's inner promptings.

> God is love,
> and he who abides in love
> abides in God,
> and God in him.
>                 (1 Jn 4:16)

---

To Read and To Do:

1. Read sections of the following Vatican II documents and report to the class:

   Decree on Ecumenism

   Declaration on the Relationship
       of the Church to Non-Christian
       Religions

   Declaration on Religious
       Freedom

2. Research what a particular Protestant denomination believes and write a one-page Credo of beliefs:

   | | | |
   |---|---|---|
   | Presbyterian | Lutheran | Episcopalian |
   | Methodist | Baptist | (Anglican) |

3. Take the Credo from exercise #2 and compare/contrast it with Catholic beliefs.

4. Research the origins of the feasts of Passover and Pentecost. Compare them to Christian belief and practice.

5. Write a Credo entitled "My Religious Beliefs":

    e.g., I believe God is good.
       I believe ....................................................
       I believe ............................................................ etc.

You may wish to illustrate this Credo with your own drawings/symbols or pictures made or cut from magazines.

6. Visit any non-Catholic church and interview the minister/rabbi, etc. Report to the class.

---

## SUMMARY

1. A strong sense of identity is needed today among Catholics.
2. The Catholic stand on right-to-life issues like abortion and euthanasia helps give Catholics a sense of standing for the helpless and defenseless. Such a stand strongly gives them an identity in a society which all too often undermines respect for life.
3. Within the Church there is a rich variety of life-styles and spiritualities which can accommodate the religious needs of Catholic youth.
4. Though the Catholic Church maintains that Jesus is accessible in the Catholic Church in a unique way, she teaches that Catholics ought to respect all religions and try to learn from them.

## EVALUATION

Finish these phrases:
    I am proud to be Catholic because ................................
    I remain a Catholic because ................................................
    The one thing I believe in as a Catholic which I would like all people to know is ................................................

# 12

## Other Questions

The format of this chapter is different from all the others in this book. It contains a number of questions and answers that have not explicitly been treated elsewhere in the book. These questions are often asked by young Catholics in their search for a deeper understanding of their faith. There is no particular order to the questions. The answers are brief and to the point. All the questions are *real* questions students have often asked the authors of this book and their colleagues. It is the hope of the authors that the answers provided are helpful to the readers.

1. *Is the rule of no marriage (celibacy) an essential requirement for the priesthood and religious life?*

The rule of celibacy, that is, deliberately and freely abstaining from marriage as a means of dedicating one's life to God, is an essential *legal* requirement for the priesthood and religious life in the Church today. The New Testament, the Fathers of the Church, early Church councils, and theology all present good reasons for a celibate priesthood, freely chosen. Some of these reasons would include Jesus' own example, the freedom to serve others without being tied down by family obligations, the witness value to all men and women that God's kingdom has broken into human history, and the like.

However, there is no theological, doctrinal or Biblical argument that would make celibacy an *obligation*. Nobody can be forced to choose a life of service which would preclude marriage.

As a matter of fact, for a long time in the Catholic Church, celibacy was not always a requirement for ordination. Even today, there are some segments of the Catholic Church which have a married clergy, for example, in some of the Eastern rites.

The law requiring priestly celibacy could be changed and if it were, it would not represent a change in doctrine or theology. If it were to change—and because of the great shortage of priests in some areas of the world, some people wish that it would change—it would be a change in a legal discipline of the Church only. Regardless of whether or not the rule of celibacy for priests is changed, celibacy will remain a valid expression of dedication and Christian discipleship. Nevertheless, Pope Paul VI has taught that there should be no change in the present discipline, nor can he see such a change in the foreseeable future.

### 2.  *Did Jesus have any brothers and sisters?*

The gospels tell us little of many of the details about Jesus' historical life. Some people (mostly in the Protestant tradition of Christianity) hold that Jesus did in fact have brothers and sisters. They point to Scripture passages like Mt 12:46-50 to support their belief.

We in the Catholic community believe, however, that Jesus did not have physical brothers and sisters. We base this belief on both Scripture and tradition. For example, the gospels (Mt 1:20 and Lk 1:34) state that Mary was a virgin and that Jesus was conceived miraculously through the power of the Holy Spirit. There is no indication in the gospels that Mary had any children after Jesus. The tradition of the Church came to look upon Mary's virginity as a symbol of God's redemptive love and power. The texts which refer to Jesus' "brothers and sisters" involve a Greek word which can also mean "cousin." Both today and in our Lord's time, people of the Near East refer to their cousins as brothers and sisters and reaffirm Mary's role as virgin. Thus, there are strong Biblical evidence and the tradition of the Church to support the conclusion that Jesus did not have brothers and sisters.

### 3.   *Was Jesus a sexual being?*

Young people have frequently asked this question in recent years because of our contemporary society's extreme interest in sex and because of the rock opera *Jesus Christ Superstar* which suggests that Jesus had physical (even marital) relations with Mary Magdalene.

Yes, Jesus was a sexual being. The mystery of the Incarnation is that God's Son assumed a human body. To be human is to be a sexual being. Jesus lived his life as a male. He had the feelings of a man. He was like us in everything, except sin. The beauty of the Incarnation is that in assuming a human nature, God elevated human nature. There is nothing dirty about being human. There is nothing evil in being a sexual being. As Genesis puts it:

> God created man in his image;
> > in the divine image he created him;
> > male and female he created them.
> > > (Gn 1:27)

God looked at everything he had made, and he found it very good.

> (Gn 1:31)

But to say that Jesus was a sexual being who was like other men (except in sin) is not to say that Jesus had sexual relations. This is not to say that sexual relations would have been demeaning for the one whom we acknowledge as Lord. Rather, it is that there is absolutely *no* Scriptural evidence that Jesus ever married. Furthermore, the strong *constant tradition* of the Christian community which goes back to the first century has always maintained (believed) that Jesus was not married. Therefore, we conclude that Jesus never had sexual relations. The veiled suggestion in *Superstar* that he did is speculative and even disrespectful. Jesus' total oneness of mind with his Father and his constant faithfulness to the Father's will are the perfect example for all Christians who wish to follow their Lord in the area of sexual morality both before and after marriage.

4. *Why does the Church forbid sexual intercourse before marriage even when the couple involved is "truly in love" and when so many in contemporary society feel that it is all right?*

The basis of any Christian moral teaching is found in Jesus' teachings in the Sermon on the Mount (Mt 5-7). In the Sermon, Jesus calls us to a fundamental conversion *(metanoia)* of our entire life from a path of sin to a path of Christian discipleship. In this conversion we express our faith in Jesus as Lord, as the one in whom are hidden the ultimate happiness and fulfillment of our life both now and in eternity. We express, as well, our desire to make Christ's attitudes our own. We embrace the conviction that any thought or action contrary to Christ's will, that is, any sin, is the source of our unhappiness and the unhappiness of others. In short, by converting (turning) to Christ we seek all things which deepen our relationship with him and others, and we shun all things which threaten that relationship. In Christian terms, this is what it means to love one another. To truly love another is to be Christlike in our thoughts and actions to the other.

Applying this to the area of sexual morality, we find in revelation and in Christian tradition the belief that sex is fundamentally good because it is created by God. Furthermore, we find that sex is created by God to be expressed within the context of married love. In married love, a man and a woman totally make a gift of themselves to each other, and in expressing this mutual self-giving by sexual intercourse, they bring children into the world. In turn, these children find in their parents the source of love, security and companionship which they need to develop into loving, self-giving adults. Thus, parents, with their children, form a family which is the basis of society as well as the soil in which the children's faith in Jesus can take root and grow.

Thus, sex before marriage is not considered to be sinful because sex is bad, but, on the contrary, because sex is so good, and because it expresses the depths of human love *which calls not only for pleasure but also for fidelity and responsibility*. The Christian, then, in striving to live according to Christ's will, avoids using sex as a toy, a diversion, or as something that is done because it feels good or fulfills passing emotional needs. Admittedly, in our society it is a struggle to maintain the high Christian ideals. In our weakness we may often fail. But the struggle is an essential one for anyone trying to live as a disciple of Jesus Christ.

### 5. *May non-Catholic Christians receive Holy Communion at a Catholic Mass?*

The way we worship can powerfully express the unity we have among ourselves as believers. This holds true for worship among separated brothers and sisters of other faiths, too. As Vatican II puts it: "In certain special circumstances, such as in prayer services for unity and during ecumenical gatherings, it is allowable, indeed desirable that Catholics join in prayer with their separated brethren" (*Decree on Ecumenism,* 8). But what about intercommunion, that is, members of Christian denominations partaking of communion in their various Churches?

Because Holy Communion is the greatest expression of unity among Christians and because the various Christian denominations are still disunified on some very basic issues, the Church teaches that intercommunion between Catholics and other Christians is *not yet normally allowed*. It is not allowed because it would express a unity of faith that does not yet exist, it would be a misuse of what the sacrament is supposed to symbolize. (We should point out, nevertheless, that some theologians think that intercommunion may help bring about desired unity because the Eucharist *creates*—as well as celebrates—unity, community. However, the current teaching of the Church does not yet normally permit it.)

There are a couple of exceptions to this general norm: First, the *Catholic Ecumenical Directory* of 1970 allows priests to give the Eucharist to non-Catholic Christians who request it in certain "emergency" situations. Second, there may be special occasions when the local bishop will permit intercommunion. It is the constant hope and prayer of all Catholics that under the guidance of the Holy

Spirit we will be brought into a unity of faith with other Christians so that one day we can eat from the one Eucharistic bread, the source of our life.

### 6. *Do angels and devils exist?*

This question arises because of the modern mentality to question the existence of spiritual realities. Even some Christians question the belief in angels and devils, explaining references to them in Scripture as metaphors or symbolic language. However, in recent years, Pope Paul VI has clarified and reaffirmed Catholic belief in the existence of angels and devils. The pope suggests a major way to answer the questions is: Did Jesus himself believe in their existence? That Jesus did is strongly supported by the New Testament. What, then, is an angel?

Angels are created persons, that is, like us they are free, knowing, loving beings created by God for union with himself. Unlike us, however, angels are pure spirits, that is, they do not have bodies. Therefore, they are not restricted by space or time. In revelation, angels are depicted as numbering in the countless thousands. Their primary functions are to worship God and serve as his messengers and our guardians. When they were created the angels were given a basic choice, similar to our choice here on earth, of either accepting or rejecting God. Those who accepted God are now in his company. Those who rejected him are now in hell as the demons or devils which, though now conquered by Christ, have the power to tempt us into rejecting God as they did.

In reading the gospels, it is obvious that the Jews of Jesus' day and Jesus himself believed in angels: The angel Gabriel announces Jesus' birth to Mary and, later, angels announce his birth to shepherds in Bethlehem. Much of Jesus' healing ministry is depicted as the casting out of devils from those possessed by them. An angel comforts Jesus in the Garden of Gethsemane. At his empty tomb, an angel announces that Jesus is risen.

In later centuries, there was much discussion and reflection about angels. Theologians like St. Bonaventure and St. Thomas

Aquinas devoted considerable energy to developing the Church's understanding of the nature and role of angels in God's plan of salvation. It is safe to say, then, that belief in angels has a strong foundation in both Scripture and Christian tradition.

Today, with our scientific mentality and with the benefits of Scripture studies we are able to stay clear of superstitious, naive or childish Christmas-card images of angels as winged creatures floating about in long flowing robes. Likewise, we can see that many instances of "diabolical possession" either as recorded in the gospels or in recent times are often due to psychological disturbances. But our scientific mentality can blind us as well to grasping the full grandeur and magnificence of God's creation which goes far beyond what our feeble senses can grasp.

7. *What is wrong with smoking pot or drinking as a way to relax with friends?*

In general, there is nothing inherently immoral about a Christian drinking alcoholic beverages as long as the drinking does not occasion any actions or attitudes which threaten the dignity of human life. We know that Jesus himself drank wine. Scripture tells us that Jesus' first miracle was that of changing water into wine at a wedding feast. As indicated above, the possible immorality of drinking begins to arise whenever it becomes in any way the cause of actions or attitudes that are destructive of our dignity as children of God.

Statistics verify that all too often alcohol can become a form of destructive escape from the pressures and challenges of daily life. This harmful use (or rather abuse) of alcohol can take the form of either isolated instances of getting drunk (in which we degrade ourselves and hurt not only ourselves but also those who love and respect us) or the more prolonged and more serious form of the alcoholic, for whom destructive drinking becomes a way of life. Some of the situations which indicate drinking is done in a destructive and therefore sinful way are: drinking so much as to degrade oneself; drinking in situations which lower inhibitions, occasioning sinful actions in the areas of sexual morality or anger; driving while drinking, thus endangering the well-being of others and yourself; letting alcohol interfere with your activities at home or school or with friends; and lying, stealing or sneaking in order to drink in disobedience to your parents.

In general, a mature Christian teenager is one who avoids two extremes: 1) He or she avoids making a "big deal" out of drinking. 2) He or she avoids an immature and dishonest attitude with self, refusing to admit that drinking can be and often is a dangerous, foolish and destructive (and therefore sinful) action both in its immediate results and long-range effects on future life.

Phrased differently, we can say that, in youth, life lies before us with the promise of achieving truly great things. We have in youth the hope and the promise of finding love and all that makes life worth living. Unlike in old age, when one can become more rigid and restricted, youth is a time for openness and flexibility in which literally anything is possible. The truth is that this openness is not only the source of the hope of youth but is also the source of great risk. We can by our foolish actions destroy our own lives. We can in youth get into actions and attitudes which later will be the source of great sorrow and loss not only to ourselves but to our loved ones as well. In this danger lies the kernel of what is most potentially sinful in all situations of teenage drinking; namely, the quality of our relationships with God and others.

What was said of drinking applies as well to smoking pot. But in reference to smoking pot one more point must be added. The effects of pot on the mind and body are as yet not completely known. The sinful potential in using pot is directly related to the extent to which medical research will show it to be destructive to mental, emotional and physical health. Lastly, it must be pointed out that a Christian does not break the civil law without serious, justifiable reason. Both the use of pot and the purchase of alcohol by minors are illegal and this illegality contributes to the moral issue of smoking pot or drinking.

One final word. All too often young people drink and "smoke up" either to conform to peer pressure ("it's the thing to do") or to escape. We should note that the Christian is one who is willing to stand alone if need be. Furthermore, the Christian tries not to use artificial means to dull his or her coping abilities with life. The Christian is one who is engaged in life to the fullest: unafraid to accept life's challenges head-on and unwilling to narcotize for temporary escape his or her God-given sense. To live a Christian life is difficult—it is a challenge. But it is a challenge worth accepting because it marks us as disciples of the One who so loved us that he was willing to die for us. (Of course, everything said here applies to adults, too.)

### 8. *What is the Church's position on divorce and remarriage?*

There are many assaults on married life in contemporary society. Like any other married couple today, Catholics find themselves subject to the same pressures and tensions which bring about the collapse of marriages and the breakdown of family life. These pressures and tensions cause much pain and suffering in the lives of those caught in the upheaval of a broken home. Divorce and remarriage present a serious challenge to the Church which cares so much for the quality of life for everyone in the world, and in particular, for the Christian trying to live a Christ-centered married life.

The Church has consistently taught and teaches today the will of Christ regarding the permanence of marriage. It sees a sacramental, consummated marriage as being indissoluble.* The Church has emphatically affirmed that the good of the husband, wife and children is best maintained by working at the marriage and keeping permanent the *marriage covenant* which reflects God's own permanent *covenant of love* with his people.

Strong scriptural evidence that God's will excluded divorce and remarriage as a solution to painful marriages is found in Mt 19:3-12 and Mk 10:1-2.

The teaching of the Church is realistic, however, in that it allows couples to live apart (separation) for grave reasons. But

---

* See Chapter V for discussion of the Sacrament of Marriage.

separation is not divorce in a sacramental marriage, nor does separation give the couple the right to remarry.

The Church is neutral regarding civil divorce—the legal termination of a marriage by a civil authority—because the divorce does not affect the permanence of a sacramental marriage. There are divorced Catholics who are members of the community in good standing. The Church accepts their civil divorce realizing it may have been necessary for legal consequences, such as eligibility for child support funds.

However, because the civil divorce does not affect the sacramental bond of marriage, those who remarry commit a serious moral offense that could be an obstacle to the reception of the sacraments.

It should be pointed out that some marriages that fail were never, in fact, true sacramental marriages. No real sacramental marriage ever existed if one or both of the partners failed to give, or were incapable of giving, true and free consent; or if one or both did not intend a real marriage, which is a union of faithful love open (at least in principle) to the procreation of children. There are a number of cases like this in the Church today. As a result, the Church can and does make a statement acknowledging (a decree of nullity) that an apparent marriage was not a genuine marriage from the start. In such cases, there is nothing to prevent the respective partners from marrying another partner, this time with free consent and intending a real Christian marriage.

Because of the seriousness of the marriage commitment and Jesus' prohibition of divorce, the Church is quite concerned with the marriage preparation of young people. The priest who witnesses and blesses the exchange of promises between the couple must make sure that the couple was adequately instructed for marriage. Marriage is a serious, lifelong commitment which is not entered into lightly. It takes work, preparation, sacrifice and a willingness to weather all kinds of storms.

9. *Can women be ordained to the priesthood?*

The question of the ordination of women to the priesthood, like all points of controversy, has two sides. On the side of those promoting the ordination of women we find first the fundamental assertion that both male and female are created by God as equally human. Both men and women are called to salvation by Christ. As St. Paul puts it, "in Christ there are neither male nor female." But, of course, God's salvation comes to us in the garb of our concrete, historical situation with all its weakness and frailty. In applying this to the Jews we note that they had a patriarchal society, that is, the men controlled the home, the state and the synagogue. Likewise, the Western cultu~e in which the Church developed down through the centuries has been—until recently—for all practical purposes, a totally male-dominated society. This male domination has continued to influence strongly the attitudes and practices of the Church including the Church's attitude toward deciding which members of the believing community are allowed to serve the Church in priestly ministry. A growing number of women (and men) in the Church today are now advocating that the time has come to acknowledge the full equality of women in the Church by allowing them to seek ordination to the priesthood.

In opposition to this position are all those who point out that Jesus never indicated that he intended women to receive ordination. He did not even include his own mother among those chosen by him to officiate at the Eucharist, preach to all nations and perform other duties associated with the priesthood. This action on the part of Christ is not simply a matter of Jewish cultural limitations but is rather an expression of the will of Christ which we are bound to preserve. Secondly, the opponents of the ordination of women stress that the long tradition of the Church strongly supports a male-only priesthood.

But this is no reflection on the dignity of women and their role in the Church. Mary, Jesus' own mother, is Mother of the Church and numerous women saints attest to the Church's high regard for women. To date, the official teaching of the Church maintains that women are not to be ordained. The reasons given immediately above are some of those used by the official teaching of the Church to support its position on this controversial topic.